Watching English Change

Learning About Language

General Editors:
Geoffrey Leech & Mick Short, Lancaster University

Already published:

Watching English Change

An Introduction to the Study of Linguistic Change in Standard Englishes in the Twentieth Century

Laurie Bauer

Longman
London and New York

Addison Wesley Longman Limited
Edinburgh Gate, Harlow,
Essex CM20 2JE, England
and Associated Companies throughout the world.

Published in the United States of America
by Addison Wesley Longman Inc, New York

First published 1994

Second impression 1997

ISBN 0–582 210895 PPR

British Library Cataloguing in Publication Data

A catalogue record for this book is available from the British Library

Library of Congress Cataloging-in-Publication Data

Bauer, Laurie, 1949-
    Watching English change : an introduction to the study of
linguistic change in standard Englishes in the twentieth century / Laurie Bauer.
        p.   cm. — (Learning about language)
    Includes bibliographical references and index.
    ISBN 0-582-21089-5
    1. English language—20th century—History.   2. English
language—20th century—Variation.   3. Linguistic change—
—History—20th century.   I. Title.   II. Series.
PE1087.B34   1994
420'.9'04—dc20   93–38602
                                                      CIP

set by 8U in Linotron Bembo 11/12pt

Transferred to digital print on demand 2001

Printed and bound in Great Britain by Antony Rowe Ltd, Eastbourne

In memory of my father, L. F. J. Bauer, 1911–89
And of my mother, J. K. Bauer, 1919–92

For them, this is not history

Contents

Preface

It is a pleasant duty, at the end of the task of composing a book, to thank those people and institutions whose help has been instrumental in ensuring the successful outcome of the project. I am pleased to be able to make the following acknowledgements for help unstintingly given. First, much of the research aimed directly at the production of this book was done while I was on sabbatical leave from Victoria University of Wellington, and the guest of the Department of Linguistics at the University of Leeds. I should like to thank both institutions for giving me the chance to carry out this work in congenial circumstances, and free from normal distractions.

Many colleagues read early drafts of some or all of the book. Their comments have been invaluable, and have led to a far more polished finished version, with far fewer glaring errors in it. In particular, I should like to thank Scott Allan, Janet Holmes, Harry Orsman, Liz Pearce, and Jack Windsor Lewis, as well as the editors of the series, Geoff Leech and Mick Short. It should be clear that none of these people is responsible for the opinions I express, and that they may not even agree with me. For statistical advice, I am indebted to Steve Haslett, of Victoria University's Institute of Statistics and Operations Research. For help with the transfer of text from one word-processing package to another, I should like to thank Mike Bennett. I am particularly indebted to my wife, Winifred, for her careful reading and correcting of the text, for her general support at all times, and for innumerable discussions of matters connected with the project at all stages of its development. Finally, I am indebted to my parents, to whom this book is dedicated, for setting me out on the route to university in the first place, and for their support and belief in what I have done over many years.

Wellington, New Zealand   Laurie Bauer
June 1993

How to use this book

This book is intended as an introductory text. It is loosely ordered from less difficult to more difficult. In particular, presentation of material in the chapters on grammatical change and sound change makes greater demands on the reader as the chapter progresses. The final chapter, in attempting to make generalizations across the data discussed in earlier chapters as well as some new data is, in parts, conceptually more advanced than the earlier chapters, which focus on observations.

Throughout the text brief questions are introduced to allow readers to check their comprehension of preceding material. Answers are also provided in nearly all such cases. Ideally, students will cover up the printed answer and attempt to provide their own before reading the suggested solution.

At the end of each chapter there are sections called Reading and References, Notes and, in some cases, Exercises. In these sections, a rather heterogeneous collection of information is presented: comments on other areas of possible change in twentieth-century English, elaboration of some of the points made in the text where the elaboration is not relevant in the development of the chapter, discussion of the precise nature of the data that was considered in the analysis of texts, suggestions for background reading on many of the topics that are covered only briefly in the text, as well as suggestions for reading from other works which consider the same or similar phenomena. Readings and notes which are directed at a particular section in the chapter are headed with the title of the section they refer to.

Where it seemed feasible (that is, in Chapters 1–5) I have also provided an 'Exercises' section. The exercises vary enormously in difficulty, and students should not undertake them without the guidance of a teacher. They have, however, been graded (see 'Symbols used' below) to indicate the easier and the harder exercises. Some of the exercises would be more suitable for class-work, where every member of the class contributes some data to be discussed by everyone. Suggested answers to these exercises are provided at the end of the book.

Symbols used

The phonetic symbols used are those of the International Phonetic Association. The particular IPA symbols used in the transcription of modern English words are explained in the 'Guide to phonetic symbols' which follows.

*   In the exercises, this symbol indicates a relatively straightforward exercise, which even beginning students should be able to attempt.

In the text, it is used sparingly to indicate sequences of words which are not part of normal usage.

In the tables, it has a sense explained in the individual table.

†   In the exercises, this symbol indicates a more challenging exercise which should only be undertaken by advanced students.

In the tables, it has a sense explained in the individual table.

~   This symbol links forms which are used as alternatives in the community.

/ /   Slashes are used to enclose transcriptions which note only contrastive elements (e.g. the symbols listed in the guide to phonetic symbols below for current English).

[ ]   Square brackets enclose transcriptions (a) which may contain phonetic detail relevant to the discussion which is not provided by transcriptions enclosed in slashes; or (b) where no claim is made about contrastiveness.

SMALL CAPITALS are used to introduce technical terms where they are defined in the text or where their definition can be deduced from the text.

italics are used in several ways in the text, including for emphasis, but the most important use is to mark letters, words, phrases or sentences cited or talked about.

Bibliographies

Three bibliographies are presented at the end of the book: a list of references, giving details of linguistic books referred to in the text; a list of lexica, in which the various dictionaries consulted are listed; and a list of sources of data, in which the literary and other sources of genuine examples cited in the text are given. The lists of lexica and sources of data are ordered alphabetically by the abbreviation used to designate the items in the text.

Guide to phonetic symbols

The following symbols are used in the phonetic transcription of English words in this book. The symbols used are the same as those used in many standard reference works for southern Standard British English.

Symbol	Key word	Symbol	Key word
ɑː	p*art*	k	*c*oo, pa*ck*
ɒ	p*o*t	l	*l*ie, pa*l*
æ	p*a*t	m	*m*y, Pa*m*
aɪ	m*y*	n	*n*igh, pa*n*
aʊ	p*ou*t	ŋ	pa*ng*
b	*b*uy, ca*b*	ɔː	port
d	*d*ie, pa*d*	ɔɪ	bo*y*
ʤ	*J*ew, sieg*e*	p	*p*ie, *p*a*p*
ð	*th*y, see*the*	r	*r*ye
e	p*e*t	s	*s*igh, cea*se*
eɪ	p*a*te	ʃ	*sh*y, ru*ch*e
eə	m*are*	t	*t*ie, pa*t*
ə	p*o*tato	ʧ	*ch*ew, pa*tch*
əʊ	m*ow*	θ	*th*igh, ru*th*
ɜː	p*er*t	uː	m*oo*
f	*f*ie, roo*f*	ʊ	p*u*t
g	*g*uy, lea*gue*	ʊə	m*oor*
h	*h*igh	v	*v*ie, lea*v*e
iː	p*ea*t	ʌ	p*u*tt
ɪ	p*i*t	w	*w*oo
ɪə	m*ere*	z	*z*oo, ru*s*e
j	*y*ou	ʒ	rou*g*e

Acknowledgements

The Publishers are grateful to the following for permission
to reproduce copyright material:

The New York Times Syndication Sales for material from
The New York Times; Times Newspapers Limited for
material from *The Times* © Times Newspapers Ltd. 1900,
1905, 1910, 1915, 1920, 1925, 1930, 1935, 1940, 1945, 1950,
1955, 1960, 1965, 1970, 1975, 1980, 1985, 1989; Cambridge
University Press and the author Peter Trudgill for Figures
1.1, 1.2 and 4.1; Solo Syndication and Literary Agency Ltd.
for material from the Daily Mail © The Daily Mail/Solo.

CHAPTER 1

Introduction

1.1 Background to this book

Many lay people think of language change as something which happened in the past, but does not happen any longer. Until recently, many people also thought of standard English as something fixed and unchanging. To such people, a book about change in current standard English (or, as we shall see, standard Englishes) is thus doubly surprising.

This book will show that English is changing today and that you can watch the changes happening around you. This first chapter deals with some of the background required before we go on to look at actual cases of change.

1.1.1 What are standard Englishes, and why is there more than one?

Most educated people appear to have a fairly clear idea about what standard English is. It is the kind of English you are expected to have to speak if you want to get a job in broadcasting, the kind of English you must be able to use in the professions, the kind of English the teachers expect you to write in schools. It does not contain double negatives such as *We haven't got no pets*; words like *done* and *seen* are exclusively past participles in standard English, not past tense forms, so that sentences such as *I done it yesterday* or *I seen her yesterday* are not part of standard English. Moreover, people feel that something either is standard English, or it is not: there are no half measures. Some people might think it is standard English to say *It was different than I had expected*, others might think it is not, but both groups would expect that there should be a single right answer to the question, which could be discovered by appeal to the proper authority (possibly *The Concise Oxford Dictionary*, or some similar publication).

There are, however, numerous problems with this view. An obvious one is that the standard changes. If the standard never changed, it would still be standard to say *Our father, which art in heaven* as in the King James version of the Bible. Nowadays, except in direct quotation, we would have to say *Our father, who is in heaven*. The seventh edition of *The Concise Oxford Dictionary* (1982) suggests that *It was different than I had expected* is *not* part of the standard, the eighth edition (1990) suggests that it *is*. We presumably do not wish to suggest that a lot of people who previously spoke standard English suddenly started speaking non-standard English in 1990 because they still said *It was different from what I had expected*. Nor would we wish to suggest that a lot of people who spoke non-standard English in 1982 started speaking standard English in 1990 for that reason. There has to be a certain amount of room for variation within a standard.

A second problem is this: people who have jobs in broadcasting, or who have jobs in the professions, do not all speak or write in the same way. Teachers do not all try to teach precisely the same form of English to their students: in Britain only about 3 per cent of the population speak with a standard accent (Trudgill and Hannah, 1982, p. 2), so most teachers cannot model the standard accent for their students, even if they use standard grammatical patterns. Even in grammar there are differences between what is normal in the North and South of England. In the North *You haven't got to eat your cabbage* may mean 'You must not eat your cabbage', while in the South it can only mean 'You are under no obligation to eat your cabbage'. If the view presented above were correct, we would have to say that people who deviate in any way from some arbitrarily chosen notion of 'correct' do not speak or write standard English, only something close to standard English. In fact, we might not be able to find anyone who speaks standard English in this narrow sense: standard English would be a fictional standard rather than a genuine variety of English. There is not necessarily any conflict here. It might be said that standard English is a variety which people like broadcasters and teachers should aim at, even if they do not attain it. We certainly know that if they fail to attain it by too wide a margin, many people write letters of complaint to broadcasting or educational authorities. The function of such complaints can be seen as an attempt to maintain and define the standard (Milroy and Milroy, 1985). But if we accept that the standard is not a single monolithic entity, but allows a certain amount of variation, then the pointlessness of some of these complaints can be easily seen.

Even if standard English is not monolithic, there are problems with defining a single standard for all dialects of English. English is spoken natively by over 300 million people all round the world, and the English used in broadcasting and the professions in, say, Washington DC is different in many ways from the English used in broadcasting and the professions in Canberra. That is, there is regional variation between varieties of English, each of which is recognized as a standard in its own sphere of influence. These spheres of influence usually (but not invariably) correspond to countries. So we might wish to distinguish between standard US English and standard Australian English, between standard New Zealand English and standard Canadian English. It is in this sense that there are a number of different standard Englishes. Certainly, these different standards have more features in common than they have distinguishing them, but they are none the less distinct. Once we accept that, it becomes an open question how many standard varieties there are in a given country, for example. Should we distinguish a standard Norwich English from a standard Nottingham English, a standard Seattle English from a standard San Francisco English, a standard Sydney English from a standard Melbourne English? In principle, there seems to be no reason why we should not. In practice though this is not done, and one reason is that these various local standards are not codified.

It seems to be widely accepted that a standard requires a certain amount of codification. There needs to be some arbiter of what is or is not standard, and this requires some description of the standard. Such descriptions come in the form of dictionaries, descriptive grammars, books for teaching the language to foreigners, books describing 'good' usage and the like. These appear to make generalizations over national rather than sub-national varieties. We find dictionaries written specifically for Canadians, South Africans or New Zealanders. We find grammars of American and of British English (by which is usually meant English English, to the exclusion of Scots, Welsh and Irish varieties). Where we find descriptions of the language of particular localities within these larger national entities, they tend to focus on usages which are not presumed to be standard, but which contrast with the standardized national usage. In this book, following this pattern, the standard Englishes which will receive most attention are standard southern British English and standard American (i.e. United States) English (these being the varieties for which the most comprehensive descriptions are available), but reference will also be made to other national standard Englishes.

Q   Can you think of things besides those listed earlier which you hear regularly but which are not part of standard English? In discussion with your class-mates, try to list five.

Who do you know who you think speaks standard English? Do you ever hear them say the things you've just listed? If so, how do you know they are not part of the standard?

A   You will probably have listed some shibboleths, like using a preposition to end a sentence up with, or using four-letter words. The chances are that the people who you think speak standard English also say these things. You may have difficulty in deciding how you know about the standard, but you probably have to make appeal to some external authority: a parent, a teacher, a dictionary, etc. If you appealed to a person as an authority, you might like to ask them how they know what is standard, and discuss the answer you receive. A dictionary or other written source represents the codification discussed earlier.

1.1.2   Do standard Englishes change?

The following passage is a remedy for wolf's-bane poisoning, written in English in the tenth century.

Gif mon þung ete, āþege buteran ond drince; se þung gewīt on þā buteran. Eft wiþ þon stande on hēafde; āslēa him mon fela scearpena on þām scancan; þonne gewīt ūt þæt ātter þurh þā scearpan.

Without special training, no-one today can read such material; it is clear that English has changed since the tenth century. A modern translation of this passage is as follows:

If you eat wolf's-bane, take butter and drink; the poisonous plant will transfer to the butter. Then stand on your head. You should be scratched many times on the shanks; then the poison will pass out through the scratches.

This is not necessarily recommended as a treatment for wolf's-bane poisoning today! Perhaps it is just as well that most people would not be able to understand the tenth-century remedy without the translation.

The English of the fourteenth century is easier to understand for the modern reader, but still requires a certain amount of training. The following passage of Middle English written by John of Trevisa (d. 1402) is a translation of a text from earlier in the fourteenth century makes this point.

Also Englyschmen, þey3 hy hadde fram þe begynnyng þre maner speche, Southeron, Northeron, and Myddel speche in þe myddel of þe lond, as hy come of þre maner people of Germania, noþeles by commyxstion and mellyng, furst wiþ Danes and afterward wiþ Normans, in menye þe contray longage ys apeyred, and som vseþ strange wlaffyng, chyteryng, harryng, and garryng grisbittyng.

This is easier to understand, but a translation (provided immediately below) is still of great help in allowing us to understand certain parts of this passage:

Also though Englishmen had from the beginning three kinds of speech, southern, northern and middle speech from the middle of the country, as they are descended from three kinds of Germanic people, and also by mixing, first with the Danes and then with the Normans, the country language has deteriorated in many, and some use strange stammering, chittering, snarling and grating gnashing of teeth.

Again, the factual accuracy of the passage is not vouched for! The passage should, however, make the point that English has changed since the Middle English period.

Parts of Shakespeare are difficult to understand for a modern audience, so English has changed since the sixteenth century. Changes can be seen in the following brief passage from Act III Scene i of *Romeo and Juliet*.

Thy head is as full of quarrelles as an egge is full of meate, and yet thy head hath bene beaten as addle as an egge for quarrelling: thou hast quarreld with a man for coffing in the streete, because hee hath wakened thy dogge that hath laine asleep in the sun. Didst thou not fall out with a taylor for wearing his new doublet before Easter, with an other, for tying his new shooes with an old riband, and yet thou wilt tuter me from quarrelling?

There are various changes to spelling obvious from this brief extract. We would today write (and say) *has* rather than *hath*, we would use *you* rather than *thou* and we would not speak of an egg being full of meat. Despite these differences, we can understand this passage without a modern translation.

Pope and Dryden tend, on the whole, to be comprehensible to modern readers. Consider the following excerpt from Pope's *A Discourse on Pastoral Poetry*, written in 1704:

If we would copy Nature, it may be useful to take this Idea along with us, that Pastoral is an image of what they call the golden age. So that we are not to describe our shepherds as shepherds at this day really are, but as they may be conceived then to have been; when the best of men followed the employment.

In the light of examples like those presented here, it is tempting to suggest that English stopped changing in the eighteenth century, and has not changed since then. After all, most of the oddities in Dickens or Thackeray can be attributed to the prosiness which characterized the period or the individuals' style rather than to a change in the language: the works of L. Durrell or M. Peake are just as odd in their own way. Compare the following passages from Dickens and Peake, which, on the surface at least, do not show any differences of language that are not differences of style:

The difference between them, in respect of age, could not exceed four years at most; but Grace, as often happens in such cases, when no mother watches over both (the Doctor's wife was dead), seemed, in her gentle care of her young sister, and in the steadiness of her devotion to her, older than she was, and more removed, in course of nature, from all competition with her, or participation, otherwise than through her sympathy and true affection, in her wayward fancies, than their ages seemed to warrant.

                                                    (*CDCB*, p. 387).

Standing immobile throughout the day, these vivid objects, with their fantastic shadows on the wall behind them shifting and elongating hour by hour with the sun's rotation, exuded a kind of darkness for all their colour. The air between them was turgid with contempt and jealousy. The craftsmen stood about like beggars, their families clustered in silent groups. They were uncouth and prematurely aged. All radiance gone.

(*MPTG*, p. 16).

(For full references, see the References section at the end of the book under 'Sources of data'.)

Tempting though it may appear to conclude that language is no longer changing, that change in English stopped two hundred years ago, this is wrong. All living languages change. This is as true of standard varieties as it is of non-standard varieties, though the rates of change may not be the same. Consequently, it seems likely that standard varieties are changing now as they have in the past. Borrowing a term from geology, Labov (1972b, p. 275) refers to this as the UNIFORMITARIAN PRINCIPLE:

We posit that the forces operating to produce linguistic change today are of the same kind and order of magnitude as those which operated in the past five or ten thousand years.

There are certainly new factors emerging, with the growth of literacy, the convergence of widespread languages, and the development of scientific vocabulary. Yet these represent minor interventions in the structure of languages. If there are relatively constant, day-to-day effects of social interaction upon grammar and phonology, the uniformitarian principle asserts that these influences continue to operate today in the same way that they have in the past.

One of the new factors which is emerging is the influence of the media, especially radio and television. However, Trudgill (1986, pp. 40–1) argues that the effect of the media is not as great as is generally believed, except in the spread of vocabulary, new idioms, and fashionable pronunciations of individual words (an example would be *dynasty*, whose pronunciation changed from /dɪnəsti/ to /daɪnəsti/ in New Zealand under the influence of the television programme *Dynasty*). Trudgill makes the point that you do not interact with the electronic media, and, he claims, it is interaction which normally leads to change in the linguistic system. Milroy and Milroy (1985, p. 30) make a point which extends this. The media, they say, can make people aware of an innovation, but cannot make them adopt it: that requires other pressures.

This book is, in a sense, devoted to a demonstration of the uniformitarian principle: changes in standard varieties of English, working in much the same way as changes attested over the past thousand years, will be exemplified again and again.

Q *There are probably pronunciations, words or expressions that you are aware of learning from TV. How many can you find?*

A Probably very few unless you include terms such as *occluded front* which you may have heard only on TV weather forecasts. On the whole, those you are aware of will be words or catch-phrases, not pronunciations or grammatical patterns (if you are not American, you may have heard sentences like *I want for you to do this* or *it's gotten dark* only on American TV programmes, but you probably don't use them). There may, of course, be other things you are not aware of, but, if Trudgill is right, they are still likely to be of the same types.

1.1.3   Why study change in standard Englishes?

Most histories of English trace the forerunners of current standard Englishes, and ignore non-standard varieties except where they coincidentally throw light on the development of the standard variety. Scholars do not seem to write histories whose primary purpose is to trace the development of Yorkshire English or the English of the outer banks of North Carolina. Also, many histories reinforce the impression that no change occurred after the eighteenth century by not discussing any later changes, possibly because information on later changes is harder to obtain. By focusing on standard Englishes, this book continues the first of these trends, but by looking at on-going changes provides compensation for the second general tendency.

In recent years, there has been a resurgence of interest in the study of language change, especially the relation between language change and other types of linguistic variation in society. This interest was stimulated by the work of Labov, but has been taken up by numerous linguists all round the world. However, nearly all this work has been concerned with language change in non-standard varieties, in the English of New York City, Detroit, Belfast, Edinburgh or Sydney. One of the aims of this book is to report on change in the standard varieties using advances in methodology achieved by the pioneering work on non-standard varieties carried out by Labov and his students.

1.1.4 Why study change in twentieth century English?

It is interesting for theoretical reasons to study change in twentieth-century standard Englishes because it represents an extension of the use of Labovian techniques to standard varieties. This, in turn, raises a number of methodological issues whose solution is not necessarily straightforward. Indeed, this book can be read as an essay in methodology. It can equally be read for the information it presents on what facets of language are changing at the moment. In this sense, it is a descriptive study, which, like all descriptive studies, has implications for linguistic theory.

The methods for studying language change are also different for the twentieth century from those used for earlier centuries. First, there has been a boom in publishing this century, which means that a far wider range of publicly available material exists for the 1900s than for previous centuries. Because a wider range of text types is accessible, more refined analysis is possible. On the other hand, the analyst of twentieth-century material runs a serious risk of being overwhelmed by the data, and has to select relevant material with great care.

Where the spoken language is concerned, the twentieth century is also the first century for which sound-recordings have been widely available. While it is not necessarily easy to obtain representative samples of a single dialect at several times throughout the century, the existence of actual speech samples itself is sufficient to revolutionize the methods of studying sound change. For earlier periods it is necessary to consider evidence such as spellings, rhymes, overt commentaries by language teachers and others, and other sporadic data of this kind.

We have just mentioned some theoretical and methodological factors that make the study of change in twentieth-century English fascinating. There are also more practical reasons for this study. It used to be the case that historical linguistics (the study of language change) was taught in universities in History of the Language classes. The student learnt about the history of English or French or German, concentrating on the facts about the stages of that particular language rather than on the principles of language change, and acquired the principles of historical linguistics more or less as a side issue. More often, now, historical linguistics is taught under the heading of Linguistics and there it is the principles of language change which are of primary importance. But the principles cannot be taught without examples, and yet it cannot be assumed in a Linguistics class that all the students are familiar with French, German or Middle English. Since the principles are assumed to be universal, it ought to be possible to exemplify them from change occurring in any language and at any period. Using twentieth-century English allows English-speaking students to come to grips with the principles without the barrier of unfamiliar data. It would, of course, be possible to write similar studies concentrating on twentieth-century standard French or German or Spanish; the choice of English for this study is dictated solely by my own interests and knowledge.

Secondly, students who are not native speakers of English, but foreign learners, are usually presented with modern English as a homogeneous entity. This homogeneity is inevitably a fiction. Moreover, it is usually a *conservative* fiction, showing the particular standard English as it was some thirty years ago or more. At elementary levels, this fiction may be beneficial rather than harmful. But at advanced levels students need to be aware that the homogeneous picture presented to them as beginners is a fiction, and also need to be able to respond appropriately to the variation that can be found in real language use. It is one of my aims in this book to shatter the illusion of homogeneity and by showing trends of development show the direction in which conservative descriptions need to be modified.

Thirdly, there is a growing trend for senior pupils in secondary schools to be encouraged to consider diachronic aspects of their language. The sources at their disposal, or their teachers' disposal, are, however, slim. This book will add to their resources. Of course, a subject like change in twentieth-century standard Englishes is a vast one. To cover it exhaustively would take several large tomes. The size of this book is thus indication in itself of how little is covered here. Rather than attempting to cover everything that might fit within the purview of the book, I have chosen to select a few topics for study. This allows reasonably detailed coverage of those few topics, but means that the topics themselves are only illustrations of a much larger phenomenon. Some hints for other places to look for change in twentieth century English are given in the Reading and References, Notes and Exercises sections which will be found at the end of every chapter.

1.2   Observing language change

Suppose you hear, as I did recently from a radio journalist, *renumeration* for *remuneration*. You will probably assume it is an error. But errors can persist and spread. What happens for example, if you hear *anenome* for *anemone*, which is very much more common? Is *anenome* an error, or has the form now changed? Is there a point at which observers can claim to have seen a change? When should dictionaries include both forms? The questions are equally impossible to answer whether we are asking about a change in the speech of a single individual or a change in 'English', especially since both forms will typically co-exist for some time in either case. In retrospect, we can say that a change took place at a certain time, but it is difficult to observe that change while it is occurring. In the change from *anemone* to *anenome*, any speaker must say one or the other; there is no half-way house. In other cases, though, intermediate forms are possible. Consider the change from Old English *hūs* /huːs/ to Modern standard English *house* /haʊs/. This pronunciation did not simply jump from one form to another, but changed almost imperceptibly over time. You can hear different stages in the continuing change if you listen to an old-fashioned upper-class Londoner, a young upper-class London, a young speaker from the Home Counties, a young Cockney, a New Zealander and an Australian saying *house*. Without proper phonetic training, you may not be able to pin down what the differences are, though you will be able to hear that they do not all sound the same. Similarly, if you could hear speakers of Old English you would be able to hear that their vowel phoneme (or distinctive speech sound) in *hūs* sounded different from that in current *house* even if you could not specify the precise changes that phoneme underwent from decade to decade. Bloomfield (1933, p. 357) summarized this in his slogan 'phonemes change'. Bloomfield (1933, p. 347) also explicitly makes the point that language change is not observable:

The process of linguistic change has never been directly observed; ... such observation, with our present facilities, is inconceivable.

Hockett (1958, p. 439) is just as firm:

No one has yet observed sound change: we have only been able to detect it via its consequences. ... A more nearly direct observation would be theoretically possible, if impractical, but any ostensible report of such an observation so far must be discredited.

Hockett's impractical method is to make accurate acoustic records of large numbers of speakers in a tight-knit community for a number of years, and to observe the sound change from the records.

More recently, however, particularly as a result of the work of linguists such as Labov and Wang, it has become clear that we can observe language change, even without Hockett's complicated technique, and that the clue to observing language change is variation. How variation and change are related will be illustrated here using standard examples from an extensive literature on this subject.

Consider an example from Trudgill (1974a; 1988) using techniques developed by Labov. This concerns a change affecting /e/ before an /l/ in Norwich, in eastern England. The change in question is one from [ɛl] to [ɜl] to [ʌl] in words like *bell*. Trudgill terms this change 'centralization'. He assigns a pronunciation like [ɛl] the index value 1, a pronunciation like [ɜl] the index value 2 and a pronunciation [ʌl] the index value 3. By adding the index values in a lot of

words and dividing by the number of tokens, he is able to
create an 'index score' for individuals. By averaging the
index scores of individuals, he can calculate an index score
for a whole group. Let us consider what Trudgill's
informants did when reading a passage aloud. Their index
scores show how centralized their pronunciations of the
relevant vowel were on average. If we plot their index score
against their year of birth, we find the pattern shown in
Figure 1.1, where the range of possible index scores runs
from 1 (no centralization, closest to [ɛl]) to 3 (maximum
possible centralization, closest to [ʌl] on all occasions). The
graph indicates that younger speakers show a greater degree
of centralization than do older speakers. In this particular

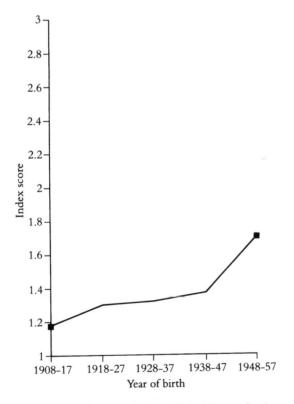

Figure 1.1 Changes to /e/ before /l/ in Norwich. From Trudgill
(1974; 1988)

case, we have further evidence that a change was taking place when the material summarized in Figure 1.1 was collected in 1968. Trudgill returned to Norwich fifteen years later, and looked at the language of the new generation of young speakers, and found the trend indicated in Figure 1.1 was continuing (Trudgill, 1988).

The change illustrated in Figure 1.1 is a change in APPARENT TIME: because older speakers show little evidence of a particular feature, and progressively younger speakers show more and more, we can hypothesize that the change is gradually becoming more established. This can be complemented by observing change in REAL TIME, as Trudgill did when he returned to Norwich fifteen years after his original survey, and carried out a new one. In effect, observing change which takes place in real time involves using Hockett's 'impractical' technique. There is a certain amount of evidence that change in apparent time is not mirrored exactly by change in real time (see, for example, Bauer, 1985, pp. 76–7), but it is generally accepted that evidence of change in apparent time does indicate that change is taking place in real time (with certain caveats which will be explored in section 1.3). So Labovian methodology allows us to observe language change by observing a pattern of variation with age.

Q *If you recorded yourself now saying the word* house *several times in different contexts, and then made a similar recording in another twenty years' time, you would probably find changes in the way you pronounce the vowel. Would that be change in apparent time or change in real time? How would you try to find evidence for the other kind of change?*

A It would be change in real time, because twenty real years would have passed between recordings. To find evidence of change in apparent time, you would make a recording of a person (or, better, a lot of people) twenty years older than you are. Differences between their speech and yours would be differences in apparent time (the apparent time being the twenty years they are older than you; all the recordings would take place in the same year).

One of the important advances that has been made by Labov and his colleagues is the demonstration that precisely the same kind of variation can be found when the conditioning factor is not time but social class or formality. One example of this is presented in Figure 1.2, with variation between /n/ and /ŋ/ in the suffix -*ing* as in *looking* in Norwich (Trudgill, 1974a, p. 92), a change sometimes misleadingly referred to as 'g-dropping' (misleading because the label refers to letters, not sounds). The range of possible scores for this data is 0–100, with 0 representing consistent use of /ŋ/ and 100 representing consistent use of /n/. Typically, people from higher social classes use forms which conform to the standard (in this case the pronunciation /ŋ/) more frequently than people from lower social classes. In Figure 1.2 this is shown by the stratification of the classes, and the non-intersection of the lines. Figure 1.2 also shows the way in which such phenomena are typically distributed across different styles. Independent of social class, people use forms which approximate more closely to the standard when they are reading than when they are talking, and use the greatest percentage of standard forms when reading lists of words (especially words which differ only in one speech sound, like *sin* and *sing*) rather than texts.

In an elaboration of this, Bell (1984, and references there) notes that the linguistic characteristics of a text are also affected by its intended audience, so that texts reflect the language of their intended audiences. This finding comes from media texts, and seems to hold in such texts for both pronunciation (in broadcast speech) and for grammatical variables.

The traditional view of the effect of social class on language change is probably that formulated by Bloomfield (1933, p. 476):

In any group, some persons receive more imitation than others; they are the leaders in power and prestige ... a speaker will imitate those whom he believes to have the highest 'social' standing.

That is, language change follows the language of the higher social classes. The work of Labov and his colleagues casts doubt on this supposition. Labov himself comments (1972b, p. 295):

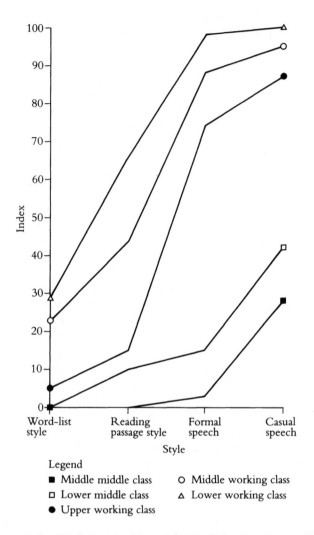

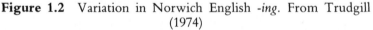

Legend
■ Middle middle class   ○ Middle working class
□ Lower middle class   △ Lower working class
● Upper working class

Figure 1.2 Variation in Norwich English -*ing*. From Trudgill (1974)

It does sometimes happen that a feature will be introduced by the highest class in the social system, though as a rule this is not an innovating group.

Rather there is evidence to show that a linguistic change can be introduced in any social class, and spread outwards from that class to others. The most frequent type is probably where a linguistic change originates with the lowest class, and spreads up the social class hierarchy. Labov (1972b, p. 290) says that

> Innovation by the highest-status group is normally a form of borrowing from outside sources, more or less conscious; with some exceptions these will be prestige forms.

or again (1972b, pp. 296–7):

> upper- and lower-class dialects innovate independently; the more conscious importations are regularly the mark of the upper class, while the less conscious changes affect both classes.

In terms of diagrams such as that in Figure 1.2, this means that the feature used most by the lowest class and least by the highest class, or the feature used most in casual speech and least in word-list style is likely to be the innovative form; exceptions arise if the innovative form has been borrowed from some other high prestige variety, and is used consciously. Note that this also implies that formal varieties of standard English are generally more conservative than less formal styles. Last year's informal usage becomes next year's formal usage.

Q *Can you think of forms from another prestige variety which have been consciously borrowed into your variety?*

A This is a hard question in the abstract. Clearly, the answer depends upon your local variety of English. In the Eastern and Southern States of the United States the answer might include pronouncing the letter *r* in words like *farm* and *shore*. In Britain and Australasia the answer might include the use of words like *flashlight*, *drapes* and *station wagon* instead of *torch*, *curtains* and *estate car*.

What counts as a prestige variety is a question which has been glossed over here. In some parts of Britain /f/ and /v/ are used at the beginnings of words like *think* and *then*, presumably in conscious imitation of Cockney, which must thus be presumed to have some kind of prestige.

Many people seem to believe that the unconscious introduction of new forms indicates laziness or slovenliness. In the *New Zealand Listener* (6 August 1977, p. 10), a correspondent berates a senior inspector of schools who was unwise enough to use 'a new word – "adaption"' on air for 'slovenly thinking' (not merely slovenly speech, note). Three weeks later (27 August 1977, pp. 10–11) a different correspondent asks 'Is it not time a protest was made about the slovenly pronunciation we hear now on both radio and television [?]' and goes on to complain that 'the way the makers of records go to so much trouble to make sure they never sound the final "g" in a word of more than one syllable is infuriating'. In the *Hutt News* of 25 March 1980, under the headline 'Sloppy speech spoiling style', the newly appointed chairman of the New Zealand Speech Board is quoted as saying New Zealanders have lazy speech habits. Such views are typical of a large group of people, and not only in New Zealand.

For this reason it is worth stating explicitly that charges of slovenliness or laziness are usually hard to uphold in cases of this type. The use of *huntin'* for *hunting* was, earlier this century, seen as characteristic of an upper-class British accent as well as a lower-class one; the variation goes back to two different forms in Old English. There are many changes, including some which start in the lowest social classes, where the innovative form takes at least as much effort to say as the conservative form. Consider the stigmatized pronunciation /drɔːrɪŋ/ for *drawing*, for example. There is no clear reason to suppose that the addition of an extra consonant in the middle of this word means that less energy is required to say it. The same stigma is attached to putting an /h/ on the beginning of a word like *eating* as to omitting the /h/ from the beginning of a word like *heating* despite the fact that if one involves the use of less energy, the other must involve the use of more energy. In a complex multiple negative such as *It ain't no cat can't get into no coop* reported by Labov, more energy is required than to say *No cat can get into the coop*. 'Slovenliness' is normally a social judgement, not a judgement of physical effort, and there are social as well as purely physical causes involved in language change.

Q   Ask some people in their sixties or older whether they are bothered by lazy or slovenly speech these days. If they answer positively, try to get them to list some features which they particularly notice. Try to work out whether the things they complain of really involve less effort to say, and why. Are these things changes?

A   Some of the things on your list will look as if they do take less effort. For instance, you will probably have been told that 'people don't open their mouths when they talk these days'. Comments of this type do not reflect changes: there have always been people complaining about others mumbling, especially if the complainers are suffering from hearing loss. If you find any real changes (the introduction of /f/ at the beginning of *think*, for example) it is usually hard to show that less effort is involved in saying the new form than in saying the old.

Change can also be observed in variation in another dimension, and that is in variation between different words. When there is a change in progress, such as the [ɛl] to [ʌl] change in Norwich, there is no guarantee that two random words such as *tell* and *elephant* will have the same index of centralization if this is calculated for the whole community. Indeed, it would be normal for one of these words to be more centralized than the other while the change was taking place. This pattern of variation between words or lexical items is called LEXICAL DIFFUSION, and its precise working will be considered in more detail in section 4.2. But because of lexical diffusion, we would not be surprised to find that individual speakers had different centralization indexes for /el/ in *tell*, *spell*, *jell*, and *Fenella*, and certainly that rare words like *meld*, *feldspar* might have a very different centralization index from the more common words. In extreme cases, it is possible for all speakers to have an innovative pronunciation in one word, while another word still retains its maximally conservative pronunciation in the speech of a large majority.

In both these cases, we can see that variation in synchronic structure (i.e. the structure at a given point of time) can be a guide to the existence of a diachronic change (i.e. change over time). It should be noted that variation in itself does not necessarily imply change, but that change is impossible without some variation. This means that variation can be taken as a clue to where there might be current change, but cannot be assumed to prove that a change is in progress (this will be illustrated more fully in section 3.4). The pattern of variation in the suffix -ing illustrated in Figure 1.2 does not appear to indicate change (Trudgill, 1988, p. 34), but it draws attention to this area as one where change could be taking place. We observe the change by observing the variation. The changing patterns of variation show a particular change making progress in a community, throughout the lexicon, and so on.

There is one guide to variation that almost always indicates change in progress: it is complaints by purists about the deterioration of the language. These sometimes take the form of letters to the editor of prestigious journals, discussions in the broadcast media or simply grouses in everyday conversation. An article like the following, which appeared in the Wellington community newspaper *Contact* (18 March 1988, p. 2) may not accurately reflect current usage, but it certainly indicates the perception of a change:

The late, magnificent Kiwi, Dame Ngaio Marsh was perpetually enraged by the inability of so many people, especially in public life, to pronounce even the simplest word correctly.

Shortly before her death, I remember talking to her at her home on the Cashmere hills about this favourite topic of hers.

'What can you do' she asked, 'when half the population pronounce the words 'men' and 'mean' the same way?'

Yet perhaps the most extraordinary thing of all is the number of people in public life who cannot even pronounce the name of their own country correctly.

It frequently emerges as 'Noo Zilln' or 'Noo Zelnd' or a kind of nasal whimper that goes merely 'Nnnnzld'.

The comment on the homophony of *men* and *mean* is factually incorrect, but it is true that people in New Zealand pronounce *men* so that it can sound like *mean* to an ear attuned to a standard English English pronunciation. What is more, this pronunciation was first remarked upon during Ngaio Marsh's lifetime, so it may well have been a change to which she was particularly sensitive. Given the constraints provided by the lack of a phonetic alphabet, the comment on the pronunciation of *New Zealand* is accurate, though its tone is unnecessarily harsh. The use of the snarl-word *whimper* to describe a normal process of reducing vowels in conversational styles shows the writer's attitude rather than anything about the supposed change itself.

The discussion in this section has been in terms of sound change, and other kinds of change have largely been ignored. However, there is every reason to suppose that the same points are valid for other types of change, except of course that lexical diffusion cannot affect lexical change. Lexical change has been shown to occur in the ways predicted by Labov (see, for example, Bayard, 1989), as has grammatical change (see, for example, Cheshire, 1978). The data in Cheshire can also be interpreted as showing that a grammatical innovation has proceeded faster with some lexical items than with others. That is, grammatical change as well as change in pronunciation can occur by lexical diffusion (see also section 6.3). In other words, the discussion of sound change in this section can be expanded, *mutatis mutandis*, to other kinds of change as well.

1.3   Predictions from observations

Dealing with on-going changes is a very hazardous undertaking. It is tempting to conclude that, because we can see the beginning of a change, it follows that the change will continue. This is not true. It may even reverse itself. Consequently, predictions based on current trends mean very little. 'If current trends continue, then we may expect to find people saying *xyz* in the year 2050' is about as risky as predicting the value of the pound or the rate of inflation. Two examples, one from French, one from English, should make the point.

Consider a change in sixteenth and seventeenth century French. In this period, the pronunciation of an intervocalic [r] (an [r] between two vowels) changed to [z]. *Mon mari est à Paris* 'My husband is in Paris' became, in effect, *Mon mazi est à Pazi*. The origin of this change is obscure, although it is said to have been a change led by the lower classes. In any case, by the early seventeenth century, there had been such a reaction against this change that [r] had been reinstated almost everywhere, and the [z] pronunciation was only a relic among some rural speakers. We might not know about this change (and thus about the reaction against it) were it not for some contemporary comments on it, and the fact that it left a handful of remnants behind. Most of the remnants are in place names, but the word *chaise* 'chair' is now distinguished from *chaire* 'pulpit, professorial chair', although they both originate in the same form. Here, then, is a case where a change was reversed almost entirely. Observers in the sixteenth century might have predicted the complete disappearance of intervocalic [r] from French, but that is not what happened: intervocalic [r] is as strong as ever. Even a well-established change need not be completed. A current English example of this will be discussed in section 4.4.

Now consider an English example. By a series of changes to vowels called the Great Vowel Shift which affected English in the sixteenth century, Middle English [oː] became [uː] in Early Modern English, which is why words spelt with *-oo-* like *bloom* are generally pronounced today with /uː/. In the seventeenth century, however, the vowel in many of these words shortened, and came to be pronounced [ʊ], the vowel sound in *could*. In the seventeenth century, pronunciations of the following words with both [uː] and [ʊ] are recorded: *cook, crook, food, foot, look, nook, rook, sooth, tooth*. Note that these include words which are now pronounced with [uː] as well as words that are now pronounced with [ʊ]. Some of these words, the ones which shortened early on, were subsequently caught up in the change which turned [ʊ] into [ʌ], the vowel sound in *cud*, except in certain environments. Thus *blood, flood* and *glove*, for example, now have [ʌ], and *look* is reported as having [ʌ] from one seventeenth century source. But the seventeenth-century change of [uː] to [ʊ] affects the modern vocabulary only sporadically. Most of the words with Middle English [oː] still have [uː] and not [ʊ]. Consider, for example, words such as: *boot, brood, cool, coop, food, goose, groom, groove, loose, moon, noon, ooze, proof, shoot, soothe, stool*. The words whose vowels shortened are in fact the minority. Here, then, we have a change which began in the seventeenth century, but which was never completed. At some stage it fizzled out, leaving us with inconsistent spelling and a few words which still allow, even in standard southern British English, two possible pronunciations, one with [uː] and the other with [ʊ]: *broom, groom, room, tooth* (Gimson, 1962, p. 112). In standard American English *hoof* and *roof* are in the same category (*PDAE*). Yet if observers in the late seventeenth century had predicted that by now everyone would be saying *coot, food* and *roost* with [ʊ], which might have seemed reasonable at the time, they would have been wrong. Perhaps equally importantly, we cannot explain why this happened, though future developments in the methods pioneered by Labov may eventually allow us to predict such cases.

Changes that are discussed in this book are changes which can be observed taking place in English in this century. There is no implication that any particular one of them will be completed, or will not reverse itself. It would be surprising if none of them were completed, but not at all surprising if some failed to be carried through.

Another trap for the unwary observer of language change is that not all linguistic changes happen at the same speed. Some appear to take place quite quickly, others may take a very long time. To make the point, consider some grammatical changes.

Current national standard varieties of English have a class of modal verbs, which are syntactically and morphologically deviant. These verbs (*can, could, will, would, shall, should, may, might, must*) do not have an infinitive (1a), an -*ing* form (1b), a past participle (1c), and do not permit a direct object (1d). We can see this by noting that the following are not possible sentences of modern English (the asterisk before them is a conventional way of indicating that they are not possible).

(1) a) ⋆I want to can go with you.
     b) ⋆After all the lessons I've had, I am canning do that.
     c) ⋆I have canned do it.
     d) ⋆I can music.

Such constructions are generally possible in other Germanic languages such as the Scandinavian languages, where the modals are much more like normal verbs (the exception is the -*ing* form, which has no equivalent in the other languages). Also, while a double modal construction was possible in earlier standard English (and is still found in some regional varieties such as Tyneside and the Southern States of America), it is no longer possible now in national standards, although it is in other Germanic languages.

(2)   *I might could get there in time.

Contrast the sentences in (1) and (2) with the Danish constructions shown in (3).

(3)   a) Jeg håber at kunne klare det. (infinitive)
           I hope to can manage it
           'I hope to be able to manage it'.
      b) Han har kunnet gøre det. (past participle)
           He has can=past.part. do it
           'He used to be able to do it'.
      c) Kan du dine tabeller? (direct object)
           Can you your tables
           'Do you know your times tables?'
      d) Jeg vil kunne nå det. (double modal)
           I will can reach it
           'I will be able to get there'.

The change away from the Germanic pattern towards the current English pattern began in the fourteenth century. Allan (1987, p. 140) dates the disappearance of the various patterns of usage with *can* and *may* as shown in Table 1.1. The date in the column for 'Direct Object', for example, shows the last date at which the type of Germanic construction illustrated in (3c) is found in standard written English. What this table shows is that the rate of change with *can* and *may* was very different, and that although the change of *may* to a modal was completed in the sixteenth century, the change of *can* to a modal was not completed until the nineteenth century. There is no particular reason why the same set of changes should have affected these two

Table 1.1   Dates of loss of grammatical patterns with two modals

Verb	Direct object	Past participle	Double modal	-ing	Infinitive
Can	1710	1587	1847	1587	1633
May	1470	1528	1532	1556	1565

Source: Allan (1987)

modals at such different rates, even less why the individual changes should have applied in different orders. Appeal to lexical diffusion here is simply labelling the case, not explaining it. It is not possible to say more than that changes do not affect all parts of a given language at the same speed.

The example of the modals shows a single set of changes affecting two similar words in the same language at different rates. It would also be possible to illustrate cases of different changes in a single language applying at very different rates, or the same change affecting different languages at different rates. Rate of change is simply not a constant, and there is currently no real explanation for this, nor any way of predicting rate of change from other factors. This clearly means that knowing the starting date of a change is not sufficient to allow anyone to predict the time at which the change will be completed.

The moral of this section is that observation of a change in progress is not a sufficient basis for making a prediction about the outcome of that change. Not only can we not predict the speed of a change, but we cannot predict whether it will be followed through to the end, or even whether it might be reversed. Diachronic linguistics is not a predictive science.

1.4   Plan of campaign

Against the theoretical background that has been established in this chapter, the next four chapters go on to establish the fact of linguistic change in twentieth century standard Englishes, giving examples of lexical changes, including changes in derivational morphology, grammatical changes (changes in inflectional morphology and syntax), sound changes (changes in phonetics and phonology), and a rather loosely titled chapter on 'Other changes' (Chapter 5). Chapter 3 on grammatical change and Chapter 4 on sound change are loosely ordered from less difficult to more difficult.

The final chapter, 'Theoretical perspective' uses the data from Chapters 2–5, and discusses problems of more theoretical interest which are raised by such data, and tries to show how linguistic theory is, to a certain extent, at least, providing explanations for the phenomena that have been observed. Since many of the explanations refer to material which is presented in different chapters, providing the theoretical aspects together in a final chapter avoids repetition, and also has the effect of separating the observation chapters from the more demanding discussion of theory.

Reading and References

1.1　Background to this book

Not many years ago it was possible to give a short and exhaustive list of the works dealing with change in the standard English of this century. Now it is virtually impossible, especially because many of the observations on this topic which have been made are to be found in books and articles ostensibly on completely different topics.

On standard languages, see, for example, Hudson (1980, pp. 32–4) and the references there. On the process of standardization, see Leith (1983) and Milroy and Milroy (1985). For discussion of linguistic change specifically in twentieth-century English (in this case, British English), see Barber (1964) and Potter (1969). While both of these are based on close observation, neither of them presents much in the way of hard evidence and they are correspondingly less academically sound than is Strang (1970). For the fact that most work in the Labovian paradigm has been concerned with non-standard forms of English, see, for example, the papers collected in Trudgill (1978). For readings on Labovian methodology in general, see below under the notes for section 1.2.

1.2　Observing language change

There are any number of introductions to (and indeed critiques of) Labovian methodology now available. One standard textbook analysis is that of Hudson (1980, ch. 5), and a slightly older one, but one concerned more particularly with the diachronic implications of Labovian theory, is Bynon (1977, ch. 5). The papers in Labov (1972a) make a good introduction in themselves.

Chambers and Trudgill (1980, pp. 174–80) provides a brief textbook introduction to lexical diffusion. Perhaps the best basic paper to read on this topic is Chen (1972). Other relevant works can be found in the bibliography to the Chen paper.

1.3 Predictions from observations

Discussion of intervocalic /r/ in French can be found in any history of the French language, although many mention it only briefly. Von Wartburg (1946, p. 156) gives quite good coverage, but dates it slightly earlier than most authorities. The account of the changes to Middle English [oː] is based on Dobson (1957), Strang (1970), Lass (1987a, p. 131) and, especially, Lass (1984, pp. 328–9), where this example is used to make the same point as in this section.

Notes for more advanced students

The notion of standard discussed in section 1.1.1 and the notion of prestige discussed in section 1.2 are very much entwined in the literature. Where graphs like those in Figures 1.1. and 1.2 are drawn, it is almost invariably found that women use more of the standard variants than men of the same age and social class do, speaking at the same style level. This has been interpreted in various ways in the literature, most of which hinge on the relationship women have with a 'prestige' form. Sometimes there is even an implication that women define prestige in language, or at least the standard. For an early discussion of these matters, see Trudgill (1974b, ch. 4), and for an insightful critique of the views expressed there and in other like-minded papers, see the papers in Part One of Coates and Cameron (1988). In most of these discussions, 'prestige' is treated as a given, while Milroy (1989) argues interestingly that it is a feature requiring explanation. In any case, if it can be used as a given, several different types of 'prestige' have to be distinguished, as many authors have noted. This means that appeals to notions of 'prestige' do not provide particularly strong arguments in the study of language change and in defining a standard, and in the present state of our ignorance are better reformulated in more measurable terms.

The evidence from Allan (1987) on the dating of modal verbs should be taken as suggestive rather than as definitive. First, Allan is arguing against a position taken by others that all the modals changed all their grammatical features within a very short period, and it is thus very much in his interests to spread the dates as much as possible. Secondly, his data comes from last listings of a particular construction in the *OED1*, which does not necessarily represent the latest time at which the construction could be used. Despite these reservations, the dates that Allan gives do appear to illustrate the point being made in the text, that changes do not always occur at the same speed. The point could no doubt be made with even greater effect by considering unlike changes, but there is always the possibility that one change takes longer than another because it affects more words, more constructions, more environments, and so on. The example of the modals rules out these possibilities.

Exercises

1.★   Consider the passages of English from different periods of history given in section 1.1.2. What things can you find, in any of these passages, that have changed today? You should consider factors such as spelling, vocabulary, and grammar.

CHAPTER 2

Lexical change

2.1 Introduction

Change in vocabulary, or lexical change, is, by its very
nature, unsystematic. Even the best descriptions of lexical
change very easily end up with lists of examples and
anecdotes, without any overview being possible. Bloomfield
and Newmark (1963) and Strang (1970) (both extremely
reputable histories of English) are able to systematize the
area of lexical change only in terms of the processes of
innovation: the various kinds of word-formation process
undergone, different kinds and sources of borrowing. This
is illuminating for the scholar who wishes to trace the
development of a particular process of word-formation, but
less so for the scholar who wants to know about the way in
which the vocabulary has developed as a whole. If an
attempt is made to give such a picture, it usually ends up
being less coherent, even in the hands of the better
practitioners of the art. Consider, for example, the following, which is an entire paragraph from Pei (1953, p. 118):

Many of our word-combinations are of recent military origin.
Some have advanced to the composition stage, where they are
spelled as one word (*blackout, dogfight, flattop, blockbuster*), others
are still felt as separate words (*scorched earth, lend-lease, walkie
talkie, swing shift*).

Remember that this passage was written soon after the
Second World War, when the point it makes was no doubt
truer than it is today. Nevertheless, it manages to raise more
questions than it answers: How many word combinations
are involved, either in real numbers or as percentages of
vocabulary? In what way are the examples typical of their

classes? Is there any common factor for the words which have 'advanced to the composition stage'?

Studies which consider change in meaning, or semantic change, do no better. We know that words change their meanings: whole books are devoted to examples of this, such as Howard (1977) or Williams (1976), for example. But while it may be possible to classify semantic changes in categories such as broadening of meanings (as when *surgical* is used of bombing to mean 'accurate' rather than 'to do with surgery, and so requiring precision') and narrowing of meanings (as when *acid*, which used to mean any acid, came, earlier this century, in some circles, to mean specifically 'lysergic acid diethylamide, LSD'), or amelioration (an improvement in meaning, as when *junkie* comes to be used for any enthusiast or devotee) and pejoration (the acquisition of a pejorative meaning, as when *turkey* comes to mean 'a stupid or inept person'), it is less clear that such distinctions are generally maintainable or that such classifications do anything more than provide useful subheadings for the textbook writer. One's answer to the question of whether the change to the word *gay*, which now means 'homosexual' but used not to mean this, and only to have the meaning 'cheerful or brightly coloured', is a case of amelioration or pejoration might depend upon one's attitude to homosexuality. But even if linguists could agree on this, *gay* does not appear to have much in common with other words which have undergone the same type of change. (Incidentally, Howard, 1977, pp. 34–6 dates this usage of *gay* from 1955 in the United States, which seems to be about the period it was starting to become generally known, although isolated examples can be found earlier than this.)

This is not to deny the fact that lexical change and innovation is widespread. Frequently, of course, it reflects change in society, as is shown by the following article which appeared in a New Zealand newspaper during 1988:

A senior citizen is one who was here before the Pill, before television, frozen food, credit cards or ball point pens. For us, time-sharing meant togetherness, not computers, and a chip meant a piece of wood. Hardwear [sic] meant hard wear, and software wasn't even a word. Teenagers never wore slacks. We were before pantyhose, drip-dry clothes, dishwashers, clothes driers and electric blankets. Girls wore Peter Pan collars and thought that cleavage was something that butchers did. We were before Batman, vitamin pills, disposable nappies, jeeps, pizzas and instant coffee, and Kentucky Fried had not even been hatched. In our day, cigarette smoking was fashionable, grass was for mowing and pot was something you cooked in. A gay person was the life and soul of the party, and nothing more, while AIDS meant beauty lotions or help for someone in trouble. We are today's senior citizens. A hardy bunch, when you think how the world has changed and of the adjustments we have had to make.

The list given here barely scratches the surface of the lexical changes which have taken place this century. To begin with, there were no *senior citizens* in New Zealand fifty years ago.

It is easy to produce similar lists from other sources. Consider the following brief list (derived from Algeo, 1991, and the second edition of the *Oxford English Dictionary*) of words and phrases which have come into English since the turn of the century.

goo smog	1900s
cartoon (film) cellophane	1910s
finalize montage	1920s
burp documentary (*noun*)	1930s
bikini car-pool	1940s
chopper 'helicopter' do-it-yourself	1950s
biodegradable brain-drain	1960s
creative accounting miniseries	1970s

$$\left.\begin{array}{c}\text{date rape} \\ \text{jetway } (\textit{or airbridge})\end{array}\right\} \quad 1980\text{s}$$

These words tell us a great deal about social history and technological progress; we may wonder how people managed without some of them; but they do not indicate any change in the language system.

Q *Consider the words listed above and see if you can decide what kinds of changes in the world have given rise to the new words. If there is no change in the world, why is there a new word? What did people say earlier?*

A Only in the case of *burp* is there no change in the world. Earlier the noun and intransitive verbs were *belch*, and the transitive verb (*to – the baby*) was *wind*. Presumably *burp* was felt to be a less impolite word than *belch*, and an appropriate-sounding word. Even in the case of *do-it-yourself*, where people had been doing things themselves for centuries, there is a change in that doing things yourself became a fashionable movement rather than a necessity.

The big problem in studies of lexical change, therefore, is looking for generalities and reproducible results. In what follows, I have made some attempt to do precisely that, although less general examples are also considered.

2.2 Changes in vocabulary sources and the makeup of words

2.2.1 Experimental method

A sample was taken from *The Supplement to the Oxford English Dictionary* (*OEDS*) (1972–86) using the following method. The single-digit number 5 was chosen at random from a table of random numbers. Every fifth word was taken from each double page of the *OEDS*, providing that

1. The word was not an addition to an entry in the first edition of the *Oxford English Dictionary* (*OED 1*).

2. The word was not spelled in precisely the same way as a word already listed in *OED 1*.

(For abbreviations of dictionary names, see under Lexica in the References at the end of the book.)

Q   *What kinds of innovation will be missed by this method?*

A   New meanings of old forms will be missed, quite deliberately. The experiment is about new forms, not about new meanings of old forms. Vocabulary change involves both of these aspects, but only one is considered here.

This gave a list of 2798 words. These words were then sorted by their date of first occurrence, according to the dictionary. Words with first citations before 1880 were discarded, since they were in some sense omissions from *OED 1*. This left a sample of 2078 words. These were divided into three groups, according to the date of first appearance: 1880–1913, 1914–38, 1939–82. 1982 represents the latest date for new words in the sample. The entire sample thus spans a century. The dates for the divisions were obviously chosen on political and not linguistic grounds. It is possible that other results would have been obtained if other dates had been used. However, one benefit that arose from choosing these politically determined dates was that they provided groups of words which were large enough to allow comparisons: there were 824 words in the first group, 613 in the second and 641 in the third.

Although the sampling procedure is perhaps not ideal, in that words on pages containing long entries stood a better chance of being selected than words on pages with only short entries, there is no obvious reason why the deviations from the ideal methodology of what statisticians call a systematic random sample should have made any difference to the results.

Using a test of statistical significance called a chi-square test, the three samples were compared on two different dimensions. First, I considered the source of the vocabulary: were the words coined from English resources or borrowed from foreign languages? Secondly, I compared the types of formations used in the words coined from English resources. Each of these will be dealt with separately below.

2.2.2   Sources of words

The words were divided into thirteen groups, according to their source, as shown in Table 2.1. Even with the amount of clustering shown in Table 2.1, some of the cells contained numbers which were rather low for statistical purposes, but further clustering was considered undesirable from a linguistic point of view. Table 2.1 shows how many words from each period fit each category, and the percentage of words from each period which come from that language or language group. The same data is presented in more approachable form in Figure 2.1. Figure 2.1 does not show, of course, the increase in the amount of word creation from English resources over the century, climbing from 68.5 per cent in the first time period to 80.8 per cent in the third, since only loans have been registered in this figure.

Statistically speaking it is clear that the distribution of words in the thirteen categories is different for each of the three time periods ($p < 0.001$, that is, there is less than one chance in a thousand that the variation shown by the three categories could arise if they were random samples from the same uniform set). The major shift in this period is an increase in the number of words created from the resources of English, and a corresponding decrease in loans, especially from French and Latin. The decrease in loans from 'other Germanic languages' and Celtic languages also contributes in an important way to the chi-square statistic, but is clearly not very important in terms of actual numbers. The large number of loans from 'other' languages in the period 1880–1913 is also important. The difference is accounted for by an influx of words from the aboriginal languages of Australia, Polynesia and the Americas. Why there should be so many of these in that particular period is an interesting question, but one which requires a historical or sociological answer, rather than a linguistic one. I shall not pursue this matter any further.

The conclusion is, therefore, that there is a decrease in the amount of borrowing of vocabulary during the twentieth century, especially from those languages which have been the main donor languages in the past.

Table 2.1 Sources of new words, 1880–1982
(observed frequencies and percentages)

Source	1880–1913	1914–38	1939–82	Total
Unknown	16	11	7	34
	1.9%	1.8%	1.1%	1.6%
English	565	476	518	1559
	68.6%	77.7%	80.8%	75.0%
French	45	22	17	84
	5.5%	3.6%	2.7%	4.0%
German	21	18	13	52
	2.5%	2.9%	2.0%	2.5%
Latin	43	22	25	90
	5.2%	3.6%	3.9%	4.3%
Greek	30	19	14	63
	3.6%	3.1%	2.2%	3.0%
Other Romance	18	11	9	38
	2.2%	1.8%	1.4%	1.8%
Other Germanic	15	11	3	29
	1.8%	1.8%	0.5%	1.4%
Slavic	6	5	7	18
	0.7%	0.8%	1.1%	0.9%
Celtic	5	2	0	7
	0.6%	0.3%	0.0%	0.3%
African (including Arabic)	14	3	8	25
	1.7%	0.5%	1.2%	1.2%
South-east Asian	9	2	8	19
	1.1%	0.3%	1.2%	0.9%
Other	37	11	12	60
	4.5%	1.8%	1.9%	2.9%
Total	824	613	641	2078
	99.9%	100.0%	100.0%	99.8%

Q Why should the main donor languages of the past no longer be such popular sources for new words as they were at the beginning of the century?

A We can only speculate; perhaps other cultures are

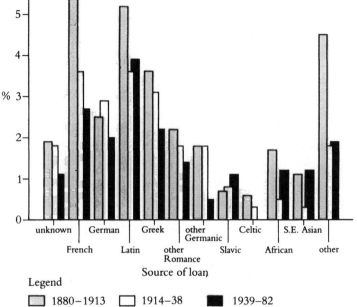

Figure 2.1   Sources of vocabulary in the twentieth century

impinging on our own these days; perhaps fewer people speak French or Latin; perhaps it is simply that more words are being coined from English elements. You may have made other suggestions, too. Some of these you can check from the data given here; others it may be possible to evaluate in terms of other data (for instance, has the number of people taking high-school French dropped in the last fifty years or so?); others it may not be possible to assess objectively. Which class do your suggestions fall into?

2.2.3   Types of formation

Words are not all formed in the same ways. The word *waitnik* is formed by adding a suffix -*nik* to a base *wait*; *de-copper* is formed by adding a prefix *de-* to a base *copper*, *executive flu* is a compound built of two words; *bibliophagic* is made up of Greek words for 'book' and 'eating' and means 'enthusiastically reading many books' – this is an English word coined from Greek elements and is a neo-classical compound; *LMS* is an abbreviation for 'local management of schools'; *rawp*, which stands for 'resource-allocation working party' is pronounced as a single syllable and is an acronym; *polyversity* is a blend of the words *polytechnic* and *university*; to *stargaze* is what is known as a back-formation from an earlier more complex *star-gazer*; *boxers* (when it is not the plural of a word for pugilist or a type of dog) is a clipped form of *boxer-shorts*; *do-wop* is onomatopoeic imitation of the musical style it names; *Ponting* ('leaking secrets to the press') is a word based on the name of Clive Ponting; words coined without any motivation, by so-called word-manufacture, such as *frug*, 'to dance', are extremely rare outside trade names (all examples from Ayto, 1990; see Bauer, 1983, for details of the types). We can call these various ways of forming words different types of formation.

Q   *Find some well-established words in each of the categories discussed above.*

The various types of formation attested in the *OEDS* were grouped together in the ten groups shown in Table 2.2. These particular groupings were chosen to be linguistically justifiable, while at the same time providing large enough figures in each cell for the statistical processes to be meaningful. 'Abbreviations' comprise both abbreviations and acronyms; 'shortenings' comprise back-formations and clippings; 'other' comprises a large group of other types of formation, including corruptions, word-manufacture, reduplication, onomatopoeic words, phrases, and so on: none of these categories was very numerous. As before, the numbers in the various categories and the percentage that each category represents of the total words coined from English sources in that period is shown in Table 2.2, and presented diagrammatically in Figure 2.2.

    This time the three distributions are significantly different at the 0.05 level, but not at the 0.01 level (that is, there is a one in twenty chance that the variation observed arises through random fluctuations in samples from a uniform whole). The main contributors to the differences are the increase in the numbers in the abbreviations category

Table 2.2 Types for formation in new words, 1880–1982
(observed frequencies and percentages)

Formation type	1880–1913	1914–38	1939–82	Total
Abbreviations	2	5	13	20
	0.4%	1.1%	2.5%	1.3%
Blends	7	14	16	37
	1.2%	2.9%	3.1%	2.4%
Shortenings	13	11	17	41
	2.3%	2.3%	3.3%	2.6%
Compounds	103	80	106	289
	18.2%	16.8%	20.5%	18.5%
Prefixation	64	62	67	193
	11.3%	13.0%	12.9%	12.4%
Suffixation	289	228	222	739
	51.2%	47.9%	42.9%	47.4%
Names	17	22	23	62
	3.0%	4.6%	4.4%	⁓4.0%
Neo-classical compounds	29	17	12	58
	5.1%	3.6%	2.3%	3.7%
Simultaneous prefix and suffix	2	2	2	6
	0.4%	0.4%	0.4%	0.4%
Other	36	33	38	114
	6.9%	7.4%	7.7%	7.3%
Total	565	476	518	1559
	100.0%	100.0%	100.0%	100.0%

and the blends category, and the decrease in the numbers in the suffixation category and the category of neo-classical compounds. Given the absolute numbers involved, the decrease in the numbers of suffixations must be considered the most important of these trends, though the increase in the non-morphological types is an interesting trend from the point of view of the student of word-formation. The compensation for this loss does not appear to come from any single type of formation, but to be spread across many. The increase in abbreviations and blends, and the non-

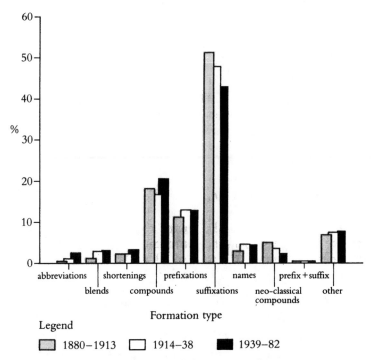

Legend

□ 1880–1913   □ 1914–38   ■ 1939–82

Figure 2.2 Processes of word-formation: changes over a century

significant increase in compounds, is not sufficient to off-set
the decrease in the proportion of suffixations.

2.2.4 Conclusion

This experiment shows that it is possible to discover trends
in vocabulary development which are independent of the
idiosyncrasies of particular technological developments or
the random changes of meaning of individual words. It is
not necessary to discuss vocabulary change in the kinds of
category mentioned in section 2.1. This is an important
principle, and the findings that have been put forward here
are just as important for supporting the principle as for the
specific results they show.

The particular results, are, of course, open to verifica-
tion from other sources. They are crucially dependent on
the criteria used by the editors of the *OEDS* for the

selection of words in that dictionary. Algeo (1980), in a random sample of 1000 words from *Barn 1*, found that approximately 30 per cent of new words were compounds. This percentage is considerably larger than the comparable figure from my data presented above. One obvious explanation is that different criteria for selection of words might have been used by the different authorities. Despite this, we must assume that the criteria for selection are consistent throughout the *OEDS* and that like has been compared with like in the experiment discussed above.

2.3   Use of the suffix *-ee*

Marchand (1969, pp. 267–8), tracing the development of the suffix *-ee* from Anglo-French into modern English, points out that the original nouns formed with this suffix were cases where

> the *-ee* sb, syntactically speaking, is ... the indirect object or prepositional object of the verb [in cases like *referee, payee*] [or] the direct object of an active verb [in cases like *nominee, appointee*].

That is, *appointee* is understood as 'someone whom somebody appointed', where *someone* is the direct object of *appoint*, while *payee* is understood as 'someone to whom somebody pays something', where *someone* is the indirect object of *pay*, or the object of the preposition *to*. Marchand also comments that cases where the derived noun is the direct object of the active verb have 'recently come into favor', and then also notes, extremely briefly, that 'A few words have a non-passive character' citing examples such as *absentee, conferee, escapee* and *standee*, which have to be understood as 'someone who is absent', and so on, where *someone* is the subject of the relative clause.

In Bauer (1983, p. 250) I commented, on the basis of very little data, that there seems in recent English to have been an increase in the non-passive meaning of the suffix. Subsequently, in Bauer (1987), I reported the arrival of a new meaning for the suffix, with nouns in *-ee* being used to denote non-humans, especially in technical terms in linguistics. We can thus observe a change in the meaning of this suffix going on in current English: we can watch semantic change taking place as it happens. This involves collecting nonce-words as they occur, rather than simply looking in dictionaries, although, of course, dictionaries remain an important source of evidence.

In order to have a basis for comparison, a survey of nineteenth century formations in -ee was made from the *OED 1*. This survey was carried out on the basis of the CD-Rom version of *OED 1*, and every word listed in the etymology as having the suffix -ee and with a first citation during the nineteenth century was extracted. There were 100 such words. All the relevant words denoted human beings. The breakdown of the words collected, in terms of the grammatical patterns they illustrated, is given in Table 2.3. The words which are listed as 'none of these' patterns in Table 2.3 are words such as *biographee*, where there is no corresponding verb, and *loanee*, which, in terms of current standard British English, looks as though it must be based on a noun, not a verb, although it might have been regularly formed from a verb in the nineteenth century.

A list of twentieth-century formations in -ee is given in Table 2.4. This set of data is not strictly comparable to the one collected for the nineteenth century. The nineteenth century corpus was collected entirely from *OED 1*. However, at the time of writing, *OED 2* is not available on CD-Rom, so that a comparable, but more up-to-date set of data is not easily obtainable. Rather, the corpus of words presented in Table 2.4 is taken partly from reference works, such as the *OEDS*, but mostly from my own reading. The sources cited are the earliest I have found. Although the majority of the words cited denote human beings, an important minority do not, and they are marked with a dagger.

Table 2.3 Nineteenth-century words using -ee

Syntactic pattern	N = %
Direct object	54
Object of a preposition	28
Subject	2
None of these	16

Source: Based on *OED 1*

Table 2.4 Words using the suffix -ee

Word	Date	Source	Example or meaning
adaptee	1971	*Barn1*	the adaptee then cannot tell the difference between yellow and white.
†advancee	1984	*PP1A*	A nominal undergoing advancement has been called an 'advancee'.
aggressee	1981	*JMFF*	Despite all the new freedoms everybody claims they have, I still feel strange when I am the aggressee.
†ascendee	1977	*AWGE*	The ascendee becomes the [Direct Object] of the matrix clause.
attendee	1976	*IAAM*	'person attending a conference'.
benefactee	1982	*DGCM*	It is typically affected by the verb, generally as benefactee or malefactee.
blackmailee	1970	*Barn1*	The relationship of the blackmailer to blackmailee.
bribee	1987	*FBAT*	We do have a line on some possible bribees.
bumpee	1980	*DFAM*	The next day the victorious bumper starts in front of the vanquished bumpee [at the Cambridge bumps].
†causee	1977	*KCNP*	The syntactic position used to encode the causee of a causative construction (i.e. the individual caused to carry out some action).
charteree	1975	*ATZB*	'person who charters a yacht, or to whom it is chartered'.
†cliticee	1987	*JADP*	Proclitics ... attach themselves to the cliticee.
cohabitee	1973	*Barn2*	A relationship between cohabitants can only survive if each cohabitee strives ...
conjuree	1983	*GMTE*	he felt less like the conjuror than the conjuree, the perplexed victim.
constipatee	1984	*SMPD*	the intent strained expressions of chronic constipatees.
contactee	1977	*LEBS*	The contactee being Miss Kerr's mother.

Table 2.4   continued

Word	Date	Source	Example or meaning
†controllee	1982	*GPGP*	A controllee is a function and a controller is either an argument ...
curee	1972	*Barn1*	The David Susskind Show pitted 'curees' against inveterate [homosexuals].
deferee	1966	*Barn1*	affluent college deferees [for the draft].
†deletee	1979	*JASM*	This principle allows deletion/ substitution only ... where the character of the deletee is ... recoverable.
†determinee	1980	*GSSL*	We can point to a reason for choosing one of the segments as determiner and the other as determinee.
†dislocatee	1983	*PPRS*	The pronominal form is a copy of the dislocatee.
drainee	1974	*LMCB*	First the brain–drain has dwindled; few potential drainees to the USA wished to be conscripted to Viet Nam.
eliminatee	1985	*PODM*	One of the eliminatees was the Chinese seaman.
explainee	1980	*RLEL*	the adoption by the explainee of the explainer's (Gricean) 'propositional attitude'.
exposee	1984	*LBTT*	Haig intended to expose a murderer, which meant that one of them was due to be the exposee.
franchisee	1968	*Barn1*	Samples ... were given to potential franchisees.
†governee	1984	*THTR*	This relation between governor and governee is regarded as a configurational property.
haulee	1985	*TPNS*	someone being hauled off to the insane asylum and an argument starts about who is insane and who is normal – hauler or haulee.

Table 2.4   continued

Word	Date	Source	Example or meaning
honoree	1980	*RDBR*	She nodded toward the six honorees and their wives.
inquisitee	1984	*RTBP*	The inquisitor becomes the inquisitee.
interrogee	1984	*WGRA*	Steve answered his own question, a trick with uncooperative interrogees.
kidnapee	1977	*AMGC*	'person kidnapped'.
knockee	1980	(*Heard*)	'Person knocking at a door'.
leakee	1976	*JETC*	He thought he could overhear the leaker and the leakee.
likee	1984	*RHIL*	The 'liker' is a male ... and ... the 'likee' is a female.
malefactee	1982	*DGCM*	(*See at* benefactee.)
manipulee	1979	*TGUG*	The manipulative speech act ... serves the ... purpose of: 1. Gaining the attention of the manipulee.
meetee	1970	*Barn1*	The meetees ... can hardly wait to get the meeting over with.
mergee	1964	*OEDS*	Such dangers as whether the mergee's inventory is all he says it is.
muggee	1972	*Barn2*	'person mugged'.
murderee	1920	*OEDS*	It takes two people to make a murder: a murderer and a murderee.
narratee	1984	*DLSW*	Is this where the narratee sits?
pleasee	1977	*FHLF*	whether John is the pleaser or pleasee.
†possessee	1982	*DGCM*	Possessive phrases in which *et* marks the subject possessee phrase.
promisee	1965	*RSPU*	An offer ... implies a quid pro quo on the part of the promisee.
pumpee	1977	*BBMM*	I decided to be the pumper [for information] not the pumpee.
puntee	1980	*DFAM*	The united cries of punters and puntees drifted from the water.

Table 2.4   continued

Word	Date	Source	Example or meaning
†reorderee	1979	*AGNC*	'Trace', which consists of . . . the categorial label and the index of the reorderee.
rescuee	1950	*OEDS*	In case of fire, no hero he; Merely a humble rescuee.
retiree	1945	*OEDS*	'a pensioner'.
returnee	1944	*OEDS*	The former hostages, already inelegantly dubbed 'returnees'.
sitee	1978	*SKTS*	How many standees and sitees we had.
slittee	1986	*JCTP*	the party gang . . . had been gung ho for slitting a few throats as long as the slittees were sound asleep.
tailee	1988	*LSTG*	The tailee walks quickly down the deserted street.
takee	1988	*LSTG*	'Firm to be taken over'.
tastee	1987	*SMCC*	this metamorphosis from taster to tastee.
tipee	1968	*Barn2*	'person receiving stock-market tip'.
torturee	1986	*JCTP*	The gifted torturer always assumes a stance of moral superiority over the torturee.
waitee	1980	*RNZ*	[In the doctor's waiting room] Sketch your fellow waitees.

† Words denoting non-humans

Q   You probably recognize very few of the words in Table 2.4. Nevertheless, some of them may seem more 'normal' to you than others. Some may strike you as being totally impossible. Go through and list them on a scale of oddness. Does your marking correspond to any structural feature of the words?

A   Your responses to these words may depend on who you are and where you live. Since they are all attested, none of them can be impossible for all speakers of English. I clearly cannot predict whether your reactions will depend on whether the noun denotes the subject or object or prepositional object of the verb, or on whether it denotes a human or non-human entity; it would not be surprising, though, if this were one factor out of several which affected your judgement.

Sixty twentieth-century words using -*ee* are listed in Table 2.4. Their adherence to the various syntactic categories is given in Table 2.5, which can be directly compared with Table 2.3. The words listed as 'Ambiguous' in Table 2.5 are all ambiguous between a subject and some other reading. They are *charteree*, *retiree* and *returnee*. It is not clear whether a *charteree* should be glossed as 'a person who charters a boat' or 'a person to whom a boat is chartered', since *charter* allows both uses. Is a *retiree* 'a person who retires' or 'a person who has been retired'? In this case, the correct gloss is probably 'a person who is retired', but that sentence is not usually understood as being passive (cp. *We have retired three workers this week*), but rather as containing an adjective. The *OEDS* glosses *returnee* as 'one who returns or is returned from abroad', where the two possible readings are given equal status. *Mergee* is another word which could be ambiguous, but I treated it as meaning 'one who a firm merges with', and being a case of object of a preposition.

From a comparison of Tables 2.3 and 2.5, it is clear that the number of -*ee* words which act syntactically as the

Table 2.5   Twentieth-century words using -*ee*

Syntactic pattern	Human *N*	Inanimate *N*	Total %
Direct object	27	10	62
Object of a preposition	7	0	12
Subject	6	1	12
None of these	6	0	10
Ambiguous	3	0	5
Total	49	11	101

Source: Based on Table 2.4.

object of a preposition is falling in this century, while the number of subject formations is on the increase. That the use of -ee to derive subject nouns is basically a twentieth-century phenomenon is confirmed by the fact that the two nineteenth-century subject formations are first attested in 1875 and 1880. The use of -ee to denote inanimate entities is not only a twentieth-century phenomenon, but a late twentieth-century phenomenon, dating from the 1970s. The earliest date for such a word in Table 2.4 is 1977, although my sources from this period imply that the words were being used earlier in the decade. For instance, an editorial note in PPRS dates an earlier version of that paper from 1972, although it cannot necessarily be assumed that dislocatee was used in that earlier version. That these words make up 18 per cent of the twentieth century corpus is astounding, even taking into account the fact that they occur in a domain (Linguistics) where I read a relatively large amount.

These two differences are so striking that they probably reflect genuine changes, despite the strict incomparability of the two bodies of data. The shift away from using -ee to derive prepositional object words is less clearly significant, but may also indicate a specialization of -ee formations.

Reading and References

2.1 Introduction

I have been unable to find the source of the article cited in section 2.1, which reached me fourth hand after having been clipped from the paper it originated in. I think it must have appeared originally in New Zealand in mid-1988.

2.2 Changes in vocabulary sources and the makeup of words

There has been a recent increase in dictionaries of new words, including Algeo (1991), Ayto (1990), *Barn 1* and *Barn 2* and dictionaries such as *The Oxford Dictionary of New Words* (ODNW) and *The Macquarie Dictionary of New Words* (MDNW), and Green (1991). It can be fascinating simply to browse through these works.

Notes

2.2   Changes in vocabulary sources and the makeup of words

In Bauer (1983, pp. 255–66) I presented a discussion of the suffix *-nik*, which showed both the rise of this suffix (or rather, of two homophonous suffixes *-nik*) and the subsequent decline in use. Although the discussion there is not primarily diachronic in nature, it can be reinterpreted as a diachronic study of the behaviour of two affixes in the course of this century. Other formatives which appear to have developed significantly during this century include *-burger, -gate, -(o)holic, -mobile, -scape, -teria, -(a)thon*. There also seems to have been a change in the use of plural attributives (*drugs courier* versus *drug courier*).

Exercises

1. Choose any of the formatives listed in the Notes section above, and look for evidence of change in the use of that formative in the course of this century. Data, and in some cases commentary, can be found in the *OEDS*, in dictionaries of new words, including *Barn 1* and *Barn 2*, and in the following specific sources (with the references they give):

    > For words with *-gate* see Algeo and Doyle (1981a) and Barnhart (1980).
    > For words with *-(o)holic*, see Algeo and Doyle (1981b) and Kolin (1979).
    > For words with *-mobile* see Aldrich (1964) and Gold (1985).
    > For words with *-scape*, see Aldrich (1966) and Gold (1977).
    > For plural attributive nouns see Dierickx (1970) and Mutt (1967).
    > Stein (1973) gives earlier references for many affixes.

2.* Take any twenty pages from one of the dictionaries of new words listed in the Reading and References section above. Try to classify the words according to whether they are loans or formed from the resources of English, and, if the latter, according to the type of formation used.

3. Choose any two of the dictionaries of new words listed in the Reading and References section above. Choose any two

letters of the alphabet, and compare and contrast the entries from the two dictionaries. Why are there differences in the word lists?

CHAPTER 3

Grammatical change

3.1 A corpus

In order to answer questions about grammatical changes which have taken place in the course of the twentieth century, I constructed a body or a CORPUS of data in the following manner. A type of data was needed which was likely to have remained fairly consistent throughout the century. The editorials or 'leading articles' in *The Times* of London seemed to fulfil this criterion. Accordingly, I chose a month at random (it happened to be March) and took the editorials for the first ten copies of *The Times* published in that month at five-yearly intervals. No Sunday papers were considered; they did not exist at the beginning of the time period. The years selected were 1900, 1905, 1910 and so on up until 1985 (1900 was, of course, not strictly speaking in the twentieth century, but this keeps the figures round ones). By this method, ten texts for each of 18 years were chosen, that is a total of 180 texts. Not all of these texts were of equal length, but even the shortest was made up of over two columns of newsprint. The amount of text considered, had it been printed in the same size of type as this book, would have covered over 500 pages.

It would be easy to find other ways of selecting appropriate data. The idea behind the system chosen was that it might allow gradual developments to be seen, while at the same time allowing a fairly large body of text from each period to be considered. It will be seen in what follows that these goals were only partly achieved. To a certain extent, this can be attributed to Murphy's Law, which applies to corpus studies as to other aspects of life. When applying to corpora, it states that a corpus will never be the right size for showing what you are trying to show: either it will be a bit too small, or it will be too big, and there will be too much data for easy analysis. The same corpus can be too small for some purposes and too large for others. This does not, however, mean that corpora are not useful in linguistic research; in many cases they are the only way of finding reliable data. What it does mean is that you have to evaluate the reliability and suitability of a particular corpus with regard to a particular point of interest when you consider the results that are obtained. The corpus taken from leading articles in *The Times* is no different from other corpora in this respect.

Other corpora of data will also be referred to in what follows, but the data from *The Times* will be referred to as *The Times* corpus.

Q   How would you go about looking for change in English grammar? Would you need a corpus of data? Why (not)? What benefits arise from using your method?

A   You would need some kind of corpus of data, though it might not be data of the same kind as that mentioned here. Even a series of anecdotes about what people used to say (and you can't assume that such anecdotes are accurate) provides data. Using a corpus of the type I used means that the data can be checked and the experiments replicated by others. It leads to relatively precise and objectively verifiable statements about change.

3.2   Comparative and superlative marking

In English there are two ways of marking the comparative and superlative of adjectives. Generally speaking, mono-syllabic adjectives (except ones like *marked, prized* which are created from participles) add the affix *-er* for the compara-tive and *-est* for the superlative: *small, smaller, smallest.* Adjectives with three or more syllables add the word *more* for the comparative, and the word *most* for the superlative: *important, more important, most important.* This leaves disyl-labic adjectives unaccounted for. Some disyllabic adjectives take *-er, -est* while others take *more, most.* Some vary between the two usages. Thus we might agree that we would probably say *happier, happiest* rather than *more happy, most happy,* (where these are genuine comparatives or superlatives: see below) and *more senseless, most senseless* rather than *senselesser, senselessest,* but we might not agree about whether we actually say *commoner, commonest* or *more common, most common.*

In dealing with such constructions, there are a few points that must be taken into account. *Most* is also used in a construction which is not a genuine superlative, in a sentence such as *That is a most interesting remark,* where *most* is equivalent to *very.* Care must be taken to keep the two constructions apart. There are also constructions with *more* and *most* which are structurally ambiguous between marking comparison and not marking comparison. Consider the following examples from *The Times* corpus. *The candidate with most valid votes* (10 March 1925) means 'with most votes which are valid' rather than 'with votes which are most valid', and is not a genuine superlative. In other examples it is impossible to tell. *The French Government is anxious to have more practical support* (10 March 1950) is ambiguous between 'support which is more practical' and 'a greater amount of support which is practical'. Again, care must be taken with such examples.

Where genuine comparatives and superlatives are concerned, both Barber (1964, p. 131) and Potter (1969, pp. 146–7) agree that, in Barber's words, '*-er* and *-est* are being replaced by forms with *more* and *most*'. Both of them agree, moreover, as to why this change is taking place. As Potter says:

This change may be seen as another manifestation of the trend from synthesis to analysis, or from complex to simple forms, which has been going on for thousands of years in the history of our language from Indo-European to modern English.

In other words, as Barber phrases it, English is losing its inflections: a complex, inflected word like *commoner* is being replaced by a sequence of simple, uninflected words like *more common.* Neither of these scholars backs these assertions up with anything other than impressions. Both cite the adjective *common* as undergoing this change; they cite only about a dozen such adjectives. As Strang (1970, p. 58) pertinently remarks:

Barber thinks there is an increasing use of *more, most*, rather than *-er, -est*, in comparison, in keeping with a trend which again goes back at least four hundred years; he may be right, but we lack precise numerical information on the subject.

Although the terms 'synthesis' and 'analysis' will be useful again later and will be used in a more general discussion in section 6.4.2, for the time being we shall avoid them, and use instead the rather more perspicuous terms 'suffixation' for a form like *commoner* and 'periphrasis' for a form like *more common*. Discussion will thus be in terms of suffixed comparison and periphrastic comparison. Apart from this change from suffixation to periphrasis in the marking of comparison on disyllabic adjectives, both Barber and Potter also comment on the increasing use of periphrasis with monosyllabic adjectives (forms like *most just*), and the increased use of periphrasis in expressions like *most well-known* rather than *best-known*. Neither of these points will be considered in the text, but there are some very brief comments in the Notes section at the end of the chapter.

At the end of the nineteenth century, Sweet (1891) reports that disyllabic adjectives which are stressed on the second syllable take the suffixed comparative, as do 'many disyllabic adjectives with the stress in the first syllable' (1891, p. 326), but that adjectives ending in *-ish, -s, -st, -ful* and *-ive* take the periphrastic comparative; all participle forms (even when monosyllabic), also take the periphrastic comparative; and disyllables stressed on the second syllable are more likely to take the periphrastic form if they end in a 'heavy consonant-group', a consonantal cluster. It will be noted that Sweet leaves a lot of room for alternatives. A grammar written in the 1980s, Quirk et al. (1985) gives a rather different picture. According to this source the monosyllabic adjectives *real, right, wrong* and *like* always take the periphrastic form; otherwise monosyllabics 'normally' take the suffixed form, but may take the periphrastic form especially in constructions such as *more – than* NP VP or *the more – the more*. Some disyllabic adjectives such as *eager* and *proper* only take the periphrastic form, but most take either, though they are more likely to take the suffixed form if they end in an unstressed vowel, syllabic /l/ or /ə^r/ (i.e. /ə/ followed by an 'r' in the spelling, which is always pronounced in some varieties of English, but is pronounced only when the next sound is a vowel in others). The use of the periphrastic form is more likely with adjectives ending in -*ly* than with those ending in -*y*.

The following disyllabic adjectives can occur with [suffixed] forms (as well as periphrastic forms, which seem to be gaining ground): *quiet, common, solid, cruel, wicked, polite, pleasant, handsome*.

(Quirk et al., 1985, p. 462)

(Both these descriptions are abbreviated and slightly simplified from their original sources, but give a good idea of the descriptions provided.)

These descriptions are very different, both in their general appearance and in their predictions. For Sweet, *likelier* is more likely than *more likely*; for Quirk et al., either might be found, with *more likely* perhaps slightly likelier! What is not clear is whether we are seeing a description of a change, or whether we are dealing with a different (and probably improved) description of the same set of facts.

The Times corpus does not give a very clear answer to questions like this. There are 17 disyllabic adjectives in that corpus which appear with both periphrastic and suffixed comparison: *ample, bitter, common, complete, costly, deadly, empty, friendly, kindly, likely, obscure, remote, robust, severe, simple, sober, wealthy*. There is some evidence of a tendency for the periphrastic comparison to be used later in the century than the suffixed comparison, but it is no more than a tendency: *wealthy*, for example, does not follow this general trend. In any case, the evidence is rather patchy, since there are more cases of comparison attested in the early years of the century than in later years. This means that in many cases suitable evidence for particular words is simply not provided by the data (see the data presented in Table 3.1). Moreover, there is no clear trend observable when all the adjectives are considered as a group. The ratio of suffixed to periphrastic comparatives for the 17 words listed above is higher in the period 1930–55 than in either the period 1900–25 or the period 1960–85. The evidence, therefore, is far from clear, with only the slightest evidence of a change towards the periphrastic comparative in the majority of those words which are attested with both forms.

In order to test whether this general trend could be

Table 3.1 Suffixed and periphrastic comparison from *The Times* corpus

17 adjectives which show both

	1900	1905	1910	1915	1920	1925	1930	1935	1940	1945	1950	1955	1960	1965	1970	1975	1980	1985
ample		★	†					★†										
bitter			†	†	†	†						★			†			
common	†		†					★†										
complete	†					★												
costly			†				★		†									
deadly				†	★†													
empty		†																
friendly							★	†	★									
kindly							★				†							
likely	†	†	†		★†	†		†		†	†							
obscure					†	★												
remote	★	★	★	†		★		★†		†					★			
robust														★				†
severe	★							†		†								
simple		★	★			★	★	★	★								†	★
sober			†						★		†							
wealthy	†												★	★		★		

Notes: ★ suffixed comparison attested
† periphrastic comparison attested

discovered in American English, and also in the hope of providing a more conclusive set of data, I carried out another experiment. This one involved reading *The New York Times* for January 1900 and January 1989. Starting with the papers of 1 January, I simply read, noting down every disyllabic adjective in the comparative or superlative, until I had collected 300 tokens from each source. This brought me to the paper of 12 January 1900, and to the end of section B in the paper of 3 January 1989. (The discrepancy is due to the increased size of the papers; both collections included a Sunday paper.) Inevitably, there will have been forms that I missed in my reading, though this should not matter a great deal. The random nature of the sample thus collected means that some adjectives simply did not occur in one or other of the samples, sometimes for obvious reasons, but more often simply by accident. For example, I think that every occurrence of the adjective *dainty* was collected from the advertisements for the department stores' January sales in 1900, and was used to refer to women's clothing; in 1989 one simply did not advertise women's clothing as being dainty. On the other hand, the fact that *remote* failed to occur in the 1989 sample is presumably purely accidental.

I shall not present the data collected in this way in a table corresponding to Table 3.1 because it was just as inconclusive. Even increasing the size of the sample to 400 tokens from each year did not add to the relevant information, and made it look likely that a corpus of over 1000 tokens for each year would be necessary to draw clear conclusions. The general tendency seen in the corpus from *The Times* could also be vaguely perceived in the data from the *New York Times*, but no more than that. The proportion of suffixed comparatives to periphrastic comparatives remained relatively constant in the two years, which suggested that there is no clear-cut switch to periphrastic comparison.

Closer examination of both the data from *The Times* corpus and from the corpus from *The New York Times* suggests, however, that the question may have been wrongly posed by scholars such as Barber and Potter. There may be an alternative, and more useful, explanation of the changes which they observe. This different pattern is observable in both The *New York Times* corpus and the *Times* corpus. Data from *The Times* corpus will be considered first.

Most of the disyllabic adjectives which take suffixed comparison end in -*y*, and most of those which take periphrastic comparison do not. In Table 3.2 a list of those adjectives which do *not* fit this generalization is provided.

Three points need to be made about the data in Table 3.2. First, all the adjectives which end in -*y* and which are attested with periphrastic comparison after 1930 in fact end in -*ly*, where that -*ly* is an adjective-forming suffix. We can therefore generalize for the latter portion of the century that the suffix -*ly* demands periphrastic comparison, but that otherwise all words ending in -*y* take suffixed comparison.

Table 3.2 Disyllabic adjectives attested in *The Times* corpus
which fail to fit the generalization about -*y*

Date	Suffixation found	Periphrasis found
1900	remote★	likely★ speedy★ wealthy★
1905	ample★ remote★ severe★ simple★	fiery likely★ worthy
1910	able humble noble remote★ simple★	costly★ likely★ risky worthy
1915		deadly★
1920	humble simple★	deadly★ likely★ lofty
1925	able complete★ narrow noble pleasant remote★ simple★	likely★ feeble
1930	obscure★ quiet simple★	weighty
1935	ample★ common★ gentle noble simple★	likely★
1940	humble remote★ sober★	friendly★
1945	humble intense	costly★ likely★

Table 3.2   continued

Date	Suffixation found	Periphrasis found
1950	humble pleasant	likely★
1955	bitter★	kindly★ likely★
1960		likely★
1965	robust★	likely★
1970	remote★	likely★
1975		
1980		
1985	simple★	likely★

Notes: Asterisked forms are also attested with the other form of comparison at some point during the century

Such a generalization does not hold before 1935. Secondly, it is striking how many of the forms with suffixed comparison end in syllabic /l/ spelled *-le*. For the latter part of the century, this is also a rule, with just one notable exception attested in 1975. Finally, note from Table 3.2 that all the words attested with suffixed comparison in breach of the primary generalization after 1950 are also attested with periphrastic comparison. It would be nice if there was clear evidence that the three relevant words in this class were moving from periphrastic to suffixed comparison, but there is no such clear data. *Bitter* is attested only once with the suffixed comparative: in 1955. *Remote* shows vacillation all through the century, but is possibly moving towards periphrastic comparison. Evidence on *robust* is too scarce to show anything, since it is only attested after 1960. What we appear to have, then, is a situation where, at the beginning of the century, there are no general rules about how to form the comparison of a disyllabic adjective. By the end of the century, the rules are becoming more fixed. Disyllabic adjectives which end in the suffix *-ly* take periphrastic comparison, other adjectives ending in *-y* and also those ending in syllabic -*le* take suffixed comparison, all others take periphrastic comparison except for a few remnants which still vacillate between the old irregular form and the new regular form.

A similar pattern emerges from *The New York Times* data. If we consider what percentage of the words showing suffixed and periphrastic comparison in 1900 and 1989 end in -*y*, we find the results given in Table 3.3. What we appear to see here is suffixed comparison becoming more and more restricted to disyllabic adjectives ending in -*y*. And if we consider the percentage of words ending in -*ly* which show suffixed and periphrastic comparison, we find the results given in Table 3.4. Here we see periphrastic comparison becoming the preferred way of making comparison for adjectives ending in the suffix -*ly*. The figures in Table 3.3 are not statistically significant, but do seem to show a trend when taken in conjunction with the other results presented here, especially since comparable figures from *The Times* corpus *are* significant. The figures in Table 3.4 *are* statistically significant ($p < 0.04$).

As another way of seeing how accurate the descriptive rules given above are for English in the 1980s, consider the

Table 3.3 Percentages of suffixed and periphrastic comparatives made up of adjectives ending in -*y* in the material from *The New York Times* (%)

	1900	1989
Suffixed	66.2	82.8
Periphrastic	5.6	3.7

Table 3.4 Percentages of suffixed and periphrastic comparatives made up of adjectives ending in -*ly* in the material from *The New York Times* (%)

	1900	1989
Suffixed	5.9	2.7
Periphrastic	5.1	7.5

following. The Wellington Corpus of Written New Zealand English comprises approximately 1.1 million running words of text written or published in New Zealand in the years 1986–90. Since New Zealand English is being described here, there is no necessary reason for it to fit generalizations based on British and American English. However, of 564 cases of comparison of disyllabic adjectives (excluding those that are -*ed* or -*ing* forms of verbs), 92 per cent fit the generalizations suggested above, only 8 per cent do not (the adjectives which do not fit include *narrow*, *quiet* and *shallow* all attested exclusively with suffixed comparison).

When I saw a bumper sticker in 1989 which announced proudly that 'I've been to the G . . . Hotel, the remotest hotel in mainland Britain' I found the suffixed comparison worthy of note; this is one of the remnants which still vacillates in general usage, though I must be (subconsciously) operating on the new rules for this word. Barber and Potter were, at an earlier stage in the century, struck by the use of *common* with an periphrastic comparative. This one has settled down into the new paradigms in the course of the century, and, indeed, is only used with periphrastic comparison in my corpus from *The New York Times*, even for 1900. Because there is still variability in the way the general rules are applied, it is possible to find both innovative and conservative forms which still sound a little unusual:

Would you care to hear my own plan just in case? It's modester but would cause less upheaval.

(*WHTM*, p. 63).

Garishest winebar for miles.

(*AATD*, p. 35).

Charlie Braine was more clever than he was given credit for.

(*ROSJ*, p. 167).

The change in the course of this century appears to have been only incidentally an increase in the use of periphrastic comparison. Rather, the change has been a regularization of a confused situation, so that it is becoming more predictable which form of comparison must be used.

Q   Put the words from Table 3.2 into invented sentences. Which sound normal, and which do not? Do your class-mates agree? Do you agree with the tentative conclusion reached in this section or not?

A   If you do not agree, see if you can formulate a better generalization. Do the words you disagree about have anything in common?

3.3   Concord with collective nouns

The agreement or CONCORD used with nouns like *government, committee* and *team* is a well-known problem of English grammar. Received wisdom on the subject is that there is 'notional concord': if the team, for example, is viewed as an entity, then singular concord is used, and we find sentences like *The team is losing its grip*; if the team is viewed as a collection of individuals, then plural concord is used and we get sentences like *The team are taking their places*. Note that these example sentences include concord with pronouns as well as verbal concord.

If the concord were purely notional, it would be expected that there would never be any linguistic change in this area, since any apparent change would have to be explained as a change in perception of teams, committees, and so on. That this is not the whole story is shown by the fact that different varieties of English use different patterns of concord with these nouns. Quirk et al. (1985, p. 19, p. 316) claim that while either singular or plural concord is possible, plural concord is used 'far less commonly in AmE than in BrE'. Either this means that American speakers all view teams as single units while British speakers are more variable in their perception of teams, governments, and so on, or, more likely, it means that the choice in this area is to some extent grammatically determined. It is under this assumption that collective nouns in *The Times* corpus were analysed with respect to the concord they show. The concord for any given noun was counted once only in any sentence except where both singular and plural concord were displayed within the same sentence.

Before the results of this analysis are presented, a warning needs to be sounded about the results. The corpus is made up of the very formal English found in the editorial columns of *The Times*. Less formal styles of writing and different contexts might give very different results. For example, there is a certain amount of evidence that in New Zealand newspaper reports, the editorial pages and the sports pages are different with respect to this variable. There is no *a priori* reason why the same should not be true of *The Times*, nor why *The Times* should not show a different pattern of variation. The results that are obtained here are thus only indicative of the state of affairs in this particular type of English. How far they can be generalized to other types of English is an open question.

Q   *If there is no change in the formal type of English which was examined in* The Times, *what if anything is this likely to mean for less formal types of English? If there is change in formal English, what if anything is it likely to imply about less formal English?*

A   If there is no change in formal English we cannot conclude anything about what is happening in less formal English. But if there is change in formal English, we would expect to find a greater degree of change in less formal English. We expect formal varieties to be the most conservative.

One of the problems of dealing with relatively limited corpora of real data is that you cannot guarantee to get the same words recurring in every time period. The noun *team*, for example, only occurs once in my data, so that no change or pattern of change emerges for that word. This is simply a failure of the data: editorials in *The Times* appear not to discuss teams very often, although they would presumably be discussed more frequently in the sports pages.

In the course of the twentieth century, in editorials from *The Times*, there appears to be an increasing tendency towards singular concord with collective nouns. This is illustrated in Figure 3.1, which shows the actual percentages recorded from my data, and also the general tendency that these very variable figures display. The tendency is statistically significant at the 1 per cent level, that is there is only one chance in a hundred that this result is due to random variation in a coherent body of data. This means

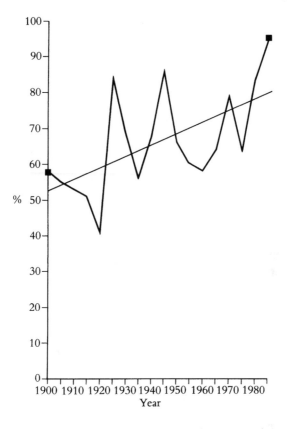

Figure 3.1   Percentage singular concord

that although it is not possible to predict with any accuracy
whether singular or plural concord will be used on any
given occasion, or even how much singular concord will be
used in any given text, there appears to be a general trend
for singular concord to increase over time. This interpretation of events is supported to some extent by the fact that it
is possible to find collective nouns which are used
exclusively with singular concord in the data (*industry*, *press*,
association, *the right*, etc.), and it is also possible to find
words which are attested with plural concord early in the
century, but only with singular concord later in the century.
For example, in *The Times* data, *army* (except in *IRA*) is last
attested with plural concord in 1900, *House* (of Commons,
of Lords) is last attested with plural concord in 1910, *enemy*

is last attested with plural concord in 1915, *Office* (home, foreign, colonial, party) is last attested with plural concord in 1920, *cabinet* is last attested with plural concord in 1940, *union* (or the name of a union) is last attested with plural concord in 1955 and so on. *Majority* and *youth* are the only recurrent collective nouns attested only with plural concord, and *majority* occurs only four times in the corpus, *youth* only twice.

By far the most frequent collective noun in this corpus is the noun *government*. As far as *government* is concerned in this corpus, a fairly clear pattern of development can be traced. This development falls into three distinct phases. Up until about 1925, *government* is used fairly freely with either singular or plural concord, plural concord being the dominant pattern. Between about 1930 and 1965 the singular and plural cases are distinguished: as a general rule, plural concord is used with the British government, and singular concord is used with foreign governments. This is not a hard and fast rule, but the numbers found are given in Table 3.5, and it can be seen that the preferred usage is the one described above, particularly in the later part of this period. In the last period, from about 1970 onwards, the preferred concord with *government* is always singular, independent of the meaning, though some traces of the earlier pattern can still be found.

Table 3.5   Concord with *government* by meaning from *The Times* corpus, 1930–65

Year	British government		Non-British government	
	Singular	Plural	Singular	Plural
1930	3	15	12	3
1935	2	13	1	12
1940	2	14	4	2
1945	2	7	2	0
1950	1	26	26	0
1955	2	2	8	0
1960	0	23	8	0
1965	1	13	4	1
Total	13	113	65	18

*Q   If what is said just above is correct, whose government would
you expect to be referred to in* The government is increasingly
being seen as out-of-touch, *if it was found in* The Times *for
1950?*

A   You would expect it to be any government except the
British government.

In the case of *government*, therefore, there is a clear
development from a state of confusion at the beginning of
the century, through a stage where the variation is
interpreted as being meaning-bearing, and finally to a stage
where the variation is decreasing in favour of grammatical
(as opposed to semantic or notional) concord.

Given that this trend is observable for the word
government, and that *government* is also the most frequent
collective noun in the corpus, it is worth considering what
the trend looks like when *government* is not included in the
data. The pattern is presented in Figure 3.2, and it is clear
that the pattern is different from that presented in Figure
3.1, which included data about *government*. In Figure 3.2
there appears to be a sudden increase in singular concord
round about 1930, with the proportions remaining fairly
constant since that time. It thus appears that the major
change in the use of singular concord occurred in the years
1925–30 approximately. There is, in the data I have
presented here, no evidence about how this change took
place (whether lexical diffusion is involved, for instance),
even less about why it took place at that time. Note,
however, that 1930 is too early for the influence of
American English to have been a major factor in this
change: most British speakers were not familiar with
American English until the Second World War or later.

*Q   Why should British speakers have become more familiar with
American English around the time of the Second World War?*

A   Many American servicemen were stationed in Britain
during the Second World War, and from that period on
there was considerable influence from films and, later,
television. Before 1939, very few people could afford to
cross the Atlantic. At the start of the war, the 'talkies' were

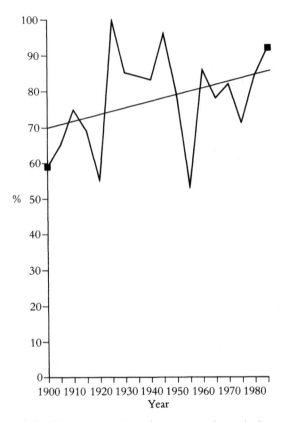

Figure 3.2 Percentage singular concord excluding the word *government*

only about ten years old. While the printed word and popular music clearly did have an effect in terms of vocabulary before that time, reactions to the speech of American servicemen in Britain during the war suggests that the effect had not been all that great in other areas, and even in the area of vocabulary had not been all-pervasive.

3.4 Relative clauses

In order to be able to consider whether there is change affecting English relative clauses, and if so what the change might be, we first need to consider in some detail the nature of relative clauses. Relative clauses, or adjectival clauses, are clauses which modify or describe nouns. The italicized clauses in (1) are relative clauses:

1. a) The girl *who saw it* let everyone know.
   b) The girl *whom I saw* wore a green beret.
   c) The girl *whose bag it was* looked very embarrassed.
   d) The bag *which I bought* wasn't as big as that.
   e) The bag *in which I put it* was blue.
   f) The bag *I put it in* was blue.
   g) The bag *that I put it in* was blue.

There are a number of features of relative clauses which need to be made explicit here.

First, there are three distinct types of relative marker in English: words which begin with *wh-* (*who*, *whom*, *whose*, *which*), as in (1a–e), the word *that*, as in (1g) and an absence of any relative marker, which we call a ZERO RELATIVE as in (1f).

Secondly, we need the term ANTECEDENT, and, using that notion, the idea of relativizing on a particular noun phrase. We analyse the sentences in (1) as containing two clauses: the matrix clause (for example *The girl let everyone know* in (1a)) and a relative clause. In all these sentences, there is one noun which is understood to play a role in both clauses, and which thus forms part of each clause. So in (1a) *the girl* is the subject of the matrix clause. Because we understand the relative clause to mean 'the girl saw it', we can say that *the girl* also functions as the subject in the relative clause, even though *the girl* has been replaced by the relative marker (*who*) in the relative clause. Now consider (1b). In this sentence *the girl* is again the subject of the matrix clause, but there the relative clause is understood to mean 'I saw the girl', where *the girl* functions as the direct object. In talking about relativization, we need two pieces of terminology: the noun which appears in the matrix clause and which is identical to the understood noun in the relative clause is called the antecedent. It goes before the relative marker and tells us what the relative marker refers to. The syntactic function of the understood noun tells us about the type of relative clause. If the understood noun is the subject of the relative clause, we have relativization on the subject; if the understood noun functions as the direct object of the relative clause, we have relativization on the direct object. Relativization on the subject complement is possible, as in

2. I very much admire the man *(that) he has become.*

but such examples are rare. All other cases of relativization are classed together in the bulk of this section as relativization on oblique noun phrases, although further subdivisions are possible and valuable for many purposes.

Thirdly, a distinction is traditionally drawn between RESTRICTIVE and NON-RESTRICTIVE (or parenthetical) relative clauses. The distinction is sometimes marked in careful writing by the use or non-use of commas, and in careful speech by the use of intonation, but this is not a reliable guide. Consider the following two examples:

3. a) The girls, who were very intelligent, played croquet well.
    b) The girls who were very intelligent played croquet well.

In (3a) all the girls we are talking about were very intelligent, and the remark on their intelligence is parenthetical to the main statement. In (3b) only those girls who were intelligent played croquet well and (implicitly) some other girls, who were not so intelligent, did not. (3a) is a non-restrictive relative clause, (3b) is a restrictive relative clause because the relative clause restricts the members of the set of girls talked about in the sentence. Standard varieties of English distinguish grammatically between the two types in that the use of *that* as a relative marker is not possible in non-restrictive clauses:

4. a) ★The girls, that were very intelligent, played croquet well.
    b) The girls that were very intelligent played croquet well.

In the bulk of this section, only restrictive relative clauses will be considered.

Finally, in oblique cases, the preposition may or may not be STRANDED. Consider the following two examples:

5. a) This is the book in which I read it.
    b) This is the book which I read it in.

In (5b) the preposition is said to be stranded at the end of the relative clause, while in (5a) the preposition has been moved to the head of the relative clause, along with the relative marker.

There are several difficulties involved in the identification of relative clauses which mean that not all scholars identify precisely the same set of clauses as being relative clauses. The distinction between restrictive and non-restrictive, mentioned above, is one such difficulty. Another factor is that the same introductory words can introduce a number of other clause types. For example, *who* and *which* also introduce indirect questions.

6. He wondered who would come.
   They didn't know which was important.

As well as introducing a variety of noun clauses as in (7a–b), *that* introduces the pseudo-cleft construction as in (7c) and clauses in apposition as in (7d).

7. a) That he is here is blindingly obvious.
   b) I know that he came.
   c) It was the lunch that made us all sick.
   d) The problem that we don't know how to begin to answer the question has held us up.

So-called 'free' relatives, where there is no overt noun for the 'relative' clauses to modify, as in

8. He knew *what he wanted*

have been ignored in the work presented here, though there might also be changes in them.

On the basis of this information, we are now in a position to give a description of the way in which relative clauses work in standard English. Crucial for the description of English relative clauses is the position which is relativized on and the human-ness of the antecedent. Where a subject is relativized on, the marker is *who* only if the antecedent is human, *which* only if the antecedent is not human, and *that* is possible under either set of circumstances. Where the direct object is relativized on, the marker is *whom* only when the antecedent is human, *which* only when the antecedent is not human, and *that* or zero under either set of circumstances. *Whose* is the relative marker for either human or non-human nouns where possession is in question. In other oblique cases, *whom* or *which* may be used, dependent on the human-ness of the antecedent, or either *that* or zero may be used. Preposition stranding is optional with *which* and *whom*, but obligatory with *that* and zero. Under appropriate semantic conditions, there is a type of incorporation of the preposition and the relative marker, and relative clauses on oblique noun phrases are found with markers *where, when, why* as in

9. The table *where he was sitting* was reserved.
    I can't remember a time *when this was not so.*
    The reason *why nobody came* was fairly obvious.

The rules given above represent a compact description of what happens in fairly formal, conservative, standard English. We turn now to consider the ways in which this pattern can be seen to be changing during the twentieth century.

Q   Which of the following sentences contain restrictive relative clauses, and in which of those is there relativization on the subject?

1. *I know who I trust.*
2. *The fact that I trust her is well-known.*
3. *This woman, who I trust implicitly, is my wife.*
4. *The person who I trust has never let me down.*
5. *Who should I trust?*
6. *The man who trusts her is wise.*

A   Only (4) and (6) contain restrictive relative clauses, and only in (6) is there relativization on the subject.

In theory, changes are possible in terms of the positions that can be relativized on, the relative markers used, the amount of preposition stranding, or in the use of particular markers with human or non-human referents. This was checked against data from *The Times* corpus, considering only the material from one year in each decade (1900, 1910, 1920, . . . 1980). There was no evidence of change on any of these parameters. There is plenty of variation, but no pattern of variation that can be interpreted as change.
    It would be possible, and even justifiable, to conclude

from this that there is no change in standard twentieth-century English in the construction of relative clauses. This could, therefore, be the end of the matter, except that this result does not match my expectations. I chose relative clauses as an area of study because, on the basis of non-systematic but informed observation over a number of years, it seemed to me that this was an area where there was change taking place. I could, of course, be wrong in my impressions, but a conclusion that there is no change at all is, for this reason, unsatisfactory to me. I note in particular that this result does not mean that no change is taking place; only that change cannot be observed in this way.

Accordingly, I constructed another corpus. This corpus was constructed by taking *The Times* and the *Daily Mail* for the entire month of September 1989 (a month chosen ahead of publication) and selecting matching stories from each paper. News, sports, editorial and television columns were used, and in the news and sports categories, reports of the same events were taken from the two papers. The editorial columns for both papers were included independent of subject, and the television columns independent of the particular programmes reviewed. Only a small number of articles from any single issue was included in the corpus, though the resultant corpus from each newspaper was fairly extensive.

Following the results obtained by Bell (1984) (see section 1.2 above), it is predicted that the language in different newspapers will vary as a function of the intended readership. It is thus predicted that the language of *The Times* will be more conservative than the language of the *Daily Mail*, since *The Times* is aimed at a higher social class than is the *Daily Mail*, and other things being equal, innovation is expected to be shown earlier in the language of lower social classes. This general point and some classes of exceptions to it were mentioned in section 1.2.

The results are disappointing in the light of my belief that there is change on-going in this area: with a corpus of 530 restrictive relative clauses from the *Daily Mail* and 807 from *The Times*, the differences between the two corpora are generally not statistically significant. The only clear difference is in terms of whether relative clauses are used to refer to humans or non-humans. The figures are presented

in Table 3.6 along with the average figures from *The Times*
corpus of leading articles for the whole century for
comparison. Now, there is, as was implied above, no
significant difference in the overall numbers of *wh-*, *that* and
zero relatives in the two September 1989 corpora. It is also
generally the case in English that a larger percentage of
relatives on subjects use *wh-* words than do relatives on
non-subjects. It thus follows that there must be a significantly larger number of non-human antecedents with
relative clauses in *wh-* in *The Times* than in the *Daily Mail*.
We must thus hypothesize that any change is a change away
from the use of *wh-* relative markers with non-human
antecedents.

The question of why there should be so many more
relative clauses on human antecedents in the *Daily Mail*
than in *The Times* is an interesting one. The most obvious
reason is that people were discussed more in the *Daily Mail*
than in *The Times*. It must be remembered, however, that a
large number of the articles dealt with the same topics. It
thus seems likely that the difference is a significant one in
terms of the styles of the two papers, and that the *Daily
Mail* chooses (almost certainly not consciously) to relativize
preferentially on human nouns. What is less clear is whether
this reflects a change in the language. It could instead be a
reflection of more basic cognitive principles. For example, it
is well-known that agents and topics tend to appear in
subject position in English, and thus tend to coincide. They
need not, but there is a tendency in this direction, no doubt
caused partially by the tendency of people towards anthro-
pocentrism. Both *The Times* and the *Daily Mail* relativize
preferentially on subjects; but if the *Daily Mail* conforms

Table 3.6 Percentages of restrictive relative clauses by human-
ness of antecedent from three sources

Source	Human	Non-human
Daily Mail, September 1989	39.4	60.6
The Times, September 1989	30.0	70.0
The Times corpus 1900–85	19.6	80.4

more closely to the tendency to have human subjects, this could account for the greater number of relative clauses on human nouns. It is still not clear whether this indicates a change in progress. Overall, it seems more likely that the difference is one of style, with a more formal style in *The Times* permitting the wider use of an unusual construction, a non-human subject. There is independent evidence that unusual structures are more common in the speech of middle-class informants (Kroch, 1978, looks at phonological instances).

What is striking about the data in Table 3.6, however, is the differences between the data for the two September, 1989 corpora and the data for *The Times* corpus of leading articles, 1900–85. Since, as has already been stated, there is no evidence of change in the 1900–85 corpus, the implication is that the differences between the 1900–85 corpus on the one hand and the 1989 corpora on the other must derive from the inclusion of less formal material alongside the formal material such as is found in editorials. If this is the case, it is in line with changes observed by others. Biesenbach-Lucas (1987, p. 18) provides the figures for zero relatives in restrictive relative clauses in *The Washington Post* reproduced in Table 3.7. What is particularly important about the figures in Table 3.7 is that they imply that there is change going on in (at least American) English with reference to the use of the zero relative marker. This change was not reflected in the difference between *The Times* and the *Daily Mail* when each newspaper was dealing with reasonably comparable topics. Percentage of zero relatives is

Table 3.7 Frequency of zero relatives in different sections of *The Washington Post* (%)

World news	0.0
Front page	2.9
Business	5.6
Letters to the editor	11.1
Style	11.8
Sports	25.0

Source: Biesenbach-Lucas (1987)

one of the parameters on which I found no significant difference.

To check this, I reanalysed the same set of data from *The Times* for September 1989, this time separating the relative clauses in editorials (except where these involved direct quotation) and relative clauses in direct quotations, that is, marked with inverted commas. The choice of editorial material was dictated by my intuition that it represented the most formal kind of writing in *The Times*. Direct quotation might be expected to be very much less formal. However, it must be borne in mind that direct quotation in a newspaper like *The Times* is not always as direct as might appear at first sight. Some of it will almost certainly have come from press releases, which were probably composed in written rather than in spoken form. Other direct quotations are ostensibly from speakers of languages other than English, in which case the words cited will represent either an interpreter's realization of the original language text, or the reporter's own translation. In all of these cases, it might be expected that the result would be more formal than genuine spoken English. It is thus likely that the figures from direct quotations in *The Times* represent figures for a more formal variety than real spoken English, and thus minimize the distance between the spoken and the editorial styles. Nevertheless, the figures, which are presented in Table 3.8 along with ranges attested in *The Times* corpus for 1900–80 for comparison, are striking. (The figures given in Table 3.8 show statistically significant differences, using a t-test, for the number of zero relatives overall, the amount of stranding, and the number of zero relatives on direct objects in the two styles in *The Times*. The figure for stranding is significant at the 0.05 level – that is there is a one in twenty chance that the difference arises simply from random fluctuations in a single coherent data set – the others at the 0.01 level or better.)

Here, then, we have clear evidence that the number of zero relatives is higher in less formal styles of British English than in more formal styles, and also that the amount of preposition stranding is greater in less formal styles. Given what we know about language change and formality, we would thus expect the increase in zero relatives and preposition stranding to be an innovative

Table 3.8   Restrictive relative clauses from *The Times*, September 1989. Editorials and direct quotations compared (%) (range from *The Times* corpus 1900–80 for comparison)

	1900–80	Editorial	Quotation
∅	1.5–8	5.9	24.0
that	6.7–17.6	17.1	17.7
wh-	66.9–90.5	77.0	58.3
stranding	0–1.8	0.9	6.3
percentage of direct objects with ∅	8–40	38.3	69.2

pattern, gradually taking over from the more explicit pattern with relative pronouns. Moreover, although Biesenbach-Lucas (1987) does not provide data on preposition stranding, her figures support the notion that the proportion of zero relatives is increasing in American English as well as in British English. In this, my results and those of Biesenbach-Lucas directly contradict the findings of Kikai et al. (1987) who conclude that 'The percentage of [zero relatives] in speech and writing is approximately the same' for a corpus of American English. This may be a reflection of the way in which their sample of relative clauses was collected, but they do not give sufficient details in their paper to be sure of this. Kikai et al. find 21 per cent of zero relatives in their data, which is high in terms of the data presented here, and may indicate that the zero relative is used more in American than in British English. They also find a far greater proportion of *that* relatives (45 per cent) than I have found in any of my data. Again, the different varieties of English sampled seem to be the most likely source of this difference. Whether there is an implication here that the proportion of *that* relatives in British English is likely to increase is not clear.

A different point, which does not emerge from the facts discussed so far, and which is difficult to pin down in text though it seems to reflect genuine user preference, is the reluctance to use *whom* to relativize on a direct object. This remains a theoretical possibility, but the single example in the Direct Quotation sample from *The Times* of September 1989 sounds distinctly odd (though possibly for reasons that have nothing to do with the use of *whom*):

Seve[riano Ballesteros] is Seve, a man not only whom you admire and respect but who has a wonderful enthusiasm for these matches.
                                   (*The Times*, 23 September 1989, p. 49, col. 1.)

The decrease in the use of *whom* marking a direct object as a percentage of all relative clauses with human antecedents in *The Times* corpus for 1900–80 and with the inclusion of the figures from 1989 is significant at the 0.05 level, but it is not clear that this is a relevant measure. Perhaps more suggestive is the fact that even in *The Times*, but also in the *Daily Mail*, alternatives with *who* replacing *whom* appear in print:

A man who others have copied but never followed; always the pacemaker, never the winner.
                                   (*Daily Mail*, 27 September 1989, p. 6, col. 1.)

All the friends and relatives who she had been with throughout her life had died.
                                   (*The Times*, 20 September 1989, p. 24, col. 4.)

Relativization on human objects tends to use zero, or, less frequently, *that*, but is not particularly common at all. In relative clauses today, *whom* is used virtually exclusively where there is relativization on obliques with no preposition stranding:

It is one that must be carefully used before it self-destructs, taking with it the people on whom Britain's future depends.
                                   (*The Times*, 7 September 1989, p. 17, col. 1.)

While this tendency to avoid *whom* for direct objects may be stronger today than it was at the beginning of the twentieth century, it has probably been noticeable throughout the century.

Q   Do you think you would use whom *in relative clauses? Do you think you would use it in questions? Would you make a distinction between speech and writing in this regard? Does it matter whether you are relativizing on direct objects or objects of prepositions?*

A   It is hard to speculate accurately about your own usage. If you are under 25, it is unlikely that you would use *whom* in speaking in anything but the most formal styles. In writing, you might use it in relative clauses, but probably only where there is relativization on the object of a preposition. You will recognize it as correct in a wider range of places than that, but probably not use it.

The movement towards preposition stranding has created an odd kind of relative clause in spoken English, where the preposition is both stranded and moved to the front of the clause:

The order in which they went to the war in. (Overheard from a professional person)

There's one thing of which you can be sure of. (Paul McCartney)

I take it that this construction indicates hesitation between the two patterns of stranding (*The order they went to the war in*) and non-stranding (*The order in which they went to the war*). If stranding becomes the norm, this construction is likely to disappear (unless it is then perceived as the correct formal version).

Strang (1970, p. 68) draws attention to the extension of zero relatives to relative clauses on subjects. I give some examples I have collected below:

It was the city gave us this job.

(*DSCT*, p. 15)

In Sugarland they know who you are.
Guess it's too late then for me. Even if I found somebody knew who I was, I wouldn't be them no more.

(*GWEM*, p. 151)

They used to arrest people did that kind of thing.

(*GVHJ*, pp. 78–9)

The doorway she used all the time . . . was a doorway used to be the front door of an olive oil company.

(*EMAP*, p. 2)

Anybody thinks they came here for their health should go back to school.

(*WDHO*, p. 39)

Such examples tend to be American and to occur in the representation of informal speech. They are thus strictly speaking outside the scope of this book, in that they do not (at least yet) represent standard English. Since such examples are common in Shakespeare's writing (Romaine, 1982, p. 5), it is, in any case, not clear whether this pattern represents a survival in non-standard English, or whether it represents an innovation. If it spreads to standard English, it will be an innovation there, even if it is a reintroduction.

There is also another pattern whose status in standard English is not yet clear, although it appears to be spreading into standard English. It is characterized by lack of agreement for human-ness between an antecedent noun and the relative marker. Where the antecedent noun is not human and *who(m)* is used, this presumably represents personification. But the use of *which* with human antecedents is also increasingly found, especially in conversation.

The first and perhaps the greatest battle for survival is fought amongst these 400 million sperms only one of whom may succeed in fertilizing the ovum.

(GBPR, p. 21)

The . . . subjects [i.e. people] which were used in the perception experiments . . .

(Student essay, New Zealand, 1979)

The result was that those First National customers which had borrowed most heavily . . . were forced under.

(PETP, pp. 13–14)

. . . slapdash attitudes of some operators which break safety rules.

(RNZ, 14 February 1990)

We have two people who live on the grounds, one of which has a dog.

(RNZ, 7 June 1990)

He told Ferranti employees which total about 24,000 in this country and abroad . . .

(The Times, 19 September 1989, p. 1, col. 7)

This pattern, like the last one, is of considerable antiquity, *which* being frequent with human antecedents until the late seventeenth century (consider the King James Bible's *Our Father, which art in Heaven*) (Romaine, 1982, p. 69). Again, it is not clear whether this pattern has always existed in non-standard forms and is being reintroduced as standard, or whether it has vanished in between times. In either case, its (re)introduction into the standard appears to be being mediated by concord with collective nouns, which can be either human or non-human (as well as either singular or plural, see above, section 3.3). An example like the following shows the confusion:

The latest petrol rise has upset the transport industry, who expects it to affect cartage rates.

(*RNZ*, November 1979)

Finally, I find that many students believe that one 'should' not use *that* with a human antecedent or *whose* with a non-human antecedent. That is, they believe that *The woman that I love* and *The house whose walls need painting* are undesirable as noun phrases. These notions apparently go back at least as far as Bishop Lowth's grammar of 1762 (Romaine, 1982, p. 134). Since any alternative to *whose* with a non-human antecedent in appropriate constructions (for example, *The house of which the walls need painting*) tends to sound clumsy, such people can usually be convinced that *whose* is possible here, even if they claim to find it awkward. There is, of course, always an alternative to *that* with a human antecedent.

In my data, *that* relative clauses never account for more than 2 per cent of relative clauses with human antecedents. It is thus clearly not normal in such cases, even if it remains grammatically possible. There is no reliable evidence of change here in the twentieth century since the numbers involved are so low, but I found no such relative clauses in the 1960, 1970, 1980 or 1989 data.

Where *whose* is concerned, again the low numbers prevent reliable conclusions. Of the tokens of *whose* in the September 1989 corpus from the *Daily Mail*, 94.4 per cent referred to humans, while only 70.6 per cent in the corresponding data from *The Times* did so, but this distinction is not statistically significant, given the small numbers involved. In the data from *The Times* corpus for 1900–80 plus the 1989 figures, there appears to be a trend towards having a smaller percentage of tokens of *whose* referring to humans. This is an area where further research might produce some interesting results, but much larger collections of data would be required if reliable answers were to be obtained, simply because of the rarity of *whose*.

Given all this, we have made a *prima facie* case in favour of change in relative clause formation during the twentieth century. In particular, we have suggested that there is a tendency to use fewer *wh-* relatives with non-human antecedents, that zero relatives correlate with less formal style (at least sometimes), that *whom* is becoming restricted in its distribution in relative clauses, and that agreement for human-ness between antecedent and relative marker may be becoming less fixed. There is a snag, though. Romaine (1982) suggests that such variation as is found here is stylistic variation, but stable; it does not indicate linguistic change.

The conclusion which can be drawn from these results is that we are dealing with variation motivated by stylistic factors, which shows considerable fluctuation, but yet has remained stable for centuries. This suggests that although rule change may begin with an increase or decrease in the probability associated with an environment, which eventually leads to a re-ordering of some of the constraints in a hierarchy, change does not necessarily occur, i.e. variation of this type does not imply change.

(Romaine, 1982, p. 204).

This conclusion is consistent with most of the evidence provided here. The implication of change is borne by our expectation that variation which is stratified in an appropriate way is a reflection of change: the expectation that variation is a symptom of change. Since variation in itself is not supposed to imply change, however, evidence which is based purely on such factors is potentially misleading, and requires close scrutiny.

In this connection, consider the data presented in Table 3.9. In this table, figures on the percentage of zero relatives, relatives with *that*, and *wh-* relatives from a number of different sources are compared. Comparable information is not available from all sources, unfortunately, so a finer breakdown is not possible.

The first thing to note from Table 3.9, looking at the data from *The Washington Post*, is that Biesenbach-Lucas (1987) does not seem to be counting the same thing as I am, when we talk about restrictive relatives. Her figures are so out of line with mine and with Romaine's that this is the only possible conclusion to draw, but in the absence of

Table **3.9** Percentages of different relative strategies in various corpora

Corpus	Ø	that	wh-
Written:			
Scottish 1† *n* not stated	0	16	84
US 1 *n* = 132	2.3	16.7	81.1
NZ *n* = 127	3.9	18.1	78.0
Scottish 2† *n* not stated	5	15	79
The Times editorials 1989 *n* = 322	5.9	17.1	77.0
US 2 *n* = 223	8	34	58
The Washington Post n = 204	8.3	56.9	34.8
GB *n* = 125	8.8	18.4	72.8
Daily Mail n = 530	9.4	15.1	75.5
Spoken:			
NZ *n* = 148	3.4	49.3	47.3
US 1 *n* = 885	16	?	?
GB 1 *n* = 145	18.6	31.0	50.3
GB 2 *n* = 1075	18.6	33.6	47.8
US 2† *n* not stated	26	56	18
US 3 *n* = 604	26	47	26
US 4 *n* = 37	29.7	43.2	27
Scottish† *n* not stated	32	60	8

Note: † = restrictive and non-restrictive clauses

Sources: Written.
Scottish 1 from *The Scotsman* (Romaine, 1982, p. 205)
NZ from a 26,000 word sample of material published ca. 1984
US 1 from a 26,000 word sample from the BROWN corpus
Scottish 2 from *The Evening Post* (Romaine, 1982, p. 205)
US 2 from academic papers in Linguistics (Guy and Bayley, 1989)
The Times and the *Daily Mail*: see earlier text
The Washington Post (Biesenbach-Lucas, 1987, p. 16)
GB from a 26,000 word sample from the LOB corpus

Spoken:
NZ from a 26,000 word sample of conversations and interviews
US 1 (Kikai et al., 1987, p. 271)
GB 1 from a 26,000 word sample from the LONDON/LUND corpus
GB 2 educated speakers (Quirk, 1957)
US 2 from interviews conducted in Philadelphia (Romaine, 1982, p. 205)
US 3 from the White House transcripts (Guy and Bailey, 1989)
US 4 (Biesenbach-Lucas, 1987, p. 16)
Scottish from interviews with teenagers and adults in Edinburgh (Romaine, 1982, p. 205)

express criteria in her article it is impossible to see what the differences might be. (Note, however, that this does not necessarily invalidate the conclusions based on the data in Table 3.7). If her figures are ignored, the other figures fall rather more into line, although the distribution of *that* and *wh-* relatives in Guy and Bayley's (1989) data (US 2) is considerably different from that in the other corpora. Perhaps the same point applies to their work. Certainly, in the other corpora, the percentage of *that* relatives is quite constant across written varieties, while the use of zero relatives does not appear to increase as a function of presumed less formal written style, though it may be related to geographical area. This definitely cannot be shown to be the case from these figures, though. The low percentage of zero relatives in the Scottish data may be a result of non-restrictive relative clauses being included in the total.

The spoken data set is harder to interpret. This is because there are differences of social class and formality hidden in the data, which it is impossible to take into account. The speakers from the LONDON/LUND corpus, for example, are nearly all academics; the New Zealand material includes speech from politicians and professional broadcasters, as well as from students and, in one case, an interview with a drugs dealer. Romaine's data is almost certainly all from people of lower socio-economic status than those in the LONDON/LUND corpus. There does, however, appear to be a marked difference between the British and New Zealand use of zero relatives. In particular, since the use of zero relatives appears generally to indicate a lesser degree of formality and/or lower social standing, it might be expected that the New Zealand data would show a higher percentage of zero relatives than the relatively formal sample of British spoken English. The contrary is the case, and this suggests a change in at least one of these varieties since about 1840, when New Zealand was first colonized by Europeans.

There is thus some evidence, albeit not very strong, that the variation in relative clause formation does reflect change, at least in some standard varieties of English. If relative clauses where the antecedent and the relative marker do not agree for human-ness are indeed becoming more frequent in otherwise standard varieties, this too may suggest change. But such change as there is during the twentieth century is certainly not dramatic.

This is not particularly surprising. Algeo (1980, p. 264) comments that

> Grammatical change . . . seems glacially slow. English speakers have been saying 'It is me' since the sixteenth century, and now, some four hundred years later, almost everybody says it, although some still don't like it.

If this common perception is true, we should not expect to find radical changes in patterns of relative clauses appearing in the last ninety years. What is important is that we can trace some change, even within this century. It thus seems that at least some of the variation in the use of relatives does indicate change. It also makes the point that slow change can be difficult to pin down, though this does not mean that we should abandon the exercise.

3.5 Methodological observations

Looking back over this chapter, one thing that emerges quite clearly is that all the constructions that have been dealt with are towards the morphological end of grammar. There are two reasons for this. The first is that it is easier to spot a morphological construction than to spot a syntactic one. This is even more obvious when computer corpora are being considered than when printed pages are being read. It is fairly easy to ask a computer to find every occurrence of the word *more*, or every word that ends in -*est* (although that will include *nest, interest* and a whole lot of other words which are not superlatives). It is much harder to ask a computer to find every noun clause. In the case of zero relatives, there would, quite literally, be nothing to ask the computer to look for! While this point is not strictly relevant for the analysis of *The Times* corpus that has been discussed in this chapter, the point needs to be made that more and more research of this kind is being done on the basis of computer analysis of machine-readable texts. Until computer parsers improve their accuracy and power, this is therefore likely to remain an important point.

The second point is that syntactic constructions do not

recur with particularly great frequency. Even the rarest of English phonemes can be expected to recur once in every thousand phonemes on average. This means, in round figures, that we might expect to hear every phoneme in just over a minute's talk, on average. At this rate, even small amounts of data provide something for analysis. Where morphology is concerned, the rate of recurrence of particular affixes drops rapidly. Some derivational affixes recur extremely infrequently. And where syntax is concerned, the rate of recurrence drops again, dramatically. Negated modals scarcely occurred in *The Times* corpus. In order to find evidence of change, a large number of tokens of the construction under consideration is required. But when the constructions recur so infrequently, this means that a large amount of text is necessary before any conclusion on change can be confirmed. It has emerged from the discussion at various points that *The Times* corpus was not really large enough. The other corpora consulted were smaller. For clear answers, corpora of several million words would be required. With corpora of that size, computer analysis becomes a necessity. Thus the size of the corpus required to provide definitive answers demands that questions be asked for which a computer can find the appropriate data.

One possible way out of this bind is to use data which has already been collected by other people. This was done in section 3.4. But some of the problems with this approach also emerged. The precise method of analysis used by others is not known (in section 3.4, two of the other corpora looked as though they might have contained data which had been counted differently from the way in which my data had been counted). The sources of the other data may not be comparable with each other. The other scholars may not have counted precisely the same thing (for example, the numbers from Romaine's work listed in section 3.4 included non-restrictive as well as restrictive relative clauses).

As if this were not enough, there are other potential sources of error. It has been seen, especially in section 3.4, that it is important to keep the style level fairly constant. This is extremely difficult to do; in many cases there may be no clear measure of what it means to keep the style level constant apart from the result of the experiment. Where style is intended to vary, it is important to make sure that it varies as intended. The material from the *Daily Mail* did not show the expected contrast with the material from *The Times* in section 3.4. The same is also true if methods of comparison are analysed in *The Times* and the *Daily Mail*. For whatever reason, it seems that the choice of the *Daily Mail* was not a good one, in terms of showing up differences of style. It is clear, of course, that the *Daily Mail* is not the British daily which provides the greatest possible contrast with *The Times* in terms of readership. *The Times* is read mainly by the middle classes (especially towards the upper end of the middle classes) and by people in the 25–45 age-group. In contrast, the readership of the *Daily Mail* comes mainly from the lower middle class and the upper working class, and it is also read by a large number of people over the age of 65 (Jucker, 1989). Papers like the *Daily Mirror* or the *Sun* would have provided a greater contrast in terms of their readership, since they are read mainly by the working classes and the young. Nevertheless, it might have been expected that the *Daily Mail* would have provided a greater contrast than we have found with *The Times*. The fact that it does not in my data may be due to an effect that is well-known to social dialectologists: the CROSS-OVER EFFECT. It is a frequent finding in social dialectology that although the variables are generally stratified, as they were for the variation between /ɪn/ and /ɪŋ/ in the suffix -*ing* that was illustrated in Figure 1.2, the class with the greatest aspirations to upward social mobility may use a larger proportion of standard forms than the social class which is immediately higher. If the language of the audience of the *Daily Mail* shows this feature, the result may be that the *Daily Mail* uses more standard (and probably, therefore, more conservative) variants than would otherwise be expected. There is no evidence that this is what is going on here, but it is one possible explanation of the observed facts. Whatever the explanation, it should be clear that the choice of material is crucial to the results obtained.

The problems of dealing with diachronic change in syntax are well-known, and account for how little work has been done in this area in comparison with diachronic phonology. The problems are intensified, however, when change within a single 90-year period is considered. As was stated at the end of section 3.4, syntactic change is generally rather slow change. This point was also illustrated with the changes to modal verbs discussed in section 1.3 and illustrated in Table 1.1. The amount of change that can be expected in any brief period is thus small. The fact that any change at all can be traced may, in fact, be extremely important, even though the results are not dramatic. It would not necessarily be surprising if a syntactic change that was taking place could not be observed at all in such a short period because there is always so much variability in language.

The result of all this is that research into grammatical change, particularly within a short period, gives results which appear far less certain than research into other kinds of change. The trends do not seem as clear, the data is more open to objections of various kinds, the results have to be hedged far more with provisos. This difference will become clear when we look at sound change in Chapter 4. Such a difference is inherent in the nature of language. Syntactic change is probably slower than phonological change *because* of the different frequencies of the constructions. It is this difference that has dictated the changes that have been considered in this chapter. The fact that some fairly clear results have been presented here is important, and the fact that they are not as clear as might be desirable should not be given too much weight.

Reading and References

3.4   Relative clauses

The topic of change in relative clauses is one in which a lot of interest has been shown. Perhaps the most thorough and important work in this area, interesting for its theoretical approach as well as its results on change, is Romaine (1982). An earlier work, although against a now out-dated theoretical background, is Klima (1964).

On the motivation for dividing relative clauses into those that relativize on subjects, objects and obliques, see Keenan and Comrie (1977). Following Keenan and Comrie, some studies of English relative clauses distinguish more positions than I have done, with interesting results (see e.g. Kikai et al., 1987). Shnukal (1981) reports on the use of zero relatives relativizing on subjects in a non-standard Australian variety.

On possible explanations for the apparent slowness of grammatical change, see Hudson (1980, p. 46). Note, however, that grammatical changes have been found and commented on earlier in this chapter.

Notes

3.2   Comparative and superlative marking

The corpus from *The New York Times* provides very few examples of periphrastic comparison with a monosyllabic adjective, except where that adjective is participial: *marked*, *skilled*, and so on. However, a significant number of those found end in a consonant cluster including a stop: *apt*, *just*, *prompt*, which suggests that this form is being used preferentially by words with a particular phonological shape. There is no evidence in either of my corpora of the use of *most well-known* instead of *best-known*, etc. These constructions appear to be found in less formal styles, including in the reporting of television journalists, for example. In very informal styles, double comparatives, such as are common in Shakespeare's English, are still regularly found in many varieties: *more heavier*, *most prettiest*. These probably have to be considered non-standard today.

General

There are reasons to suspect that the use of the subjunctive is also subject to change, but it was not possible to show this from *The Times* corpus. For a full discussion of this, not only would it be necessary to find the places where subjunctives are used, but also all the places where they might have been used, but are not. Since it is much harder to spot things which are not there than things which are, this was not attempted.

Potter (1969) suggests that the future with *going to* is increasing in the twentieth century. There was simply not enough evidence in *The Times* corpus to indicate whether or not this is true. *Going to* expressing future time hardly ever occurred. Similar comments hold for the negatives of modals, especially semi–modals such as *dare, need, ought to, used to*. A far larger data base would be required to tell whether there was any change there in the twentieth century, although we may suspect that there is some change in these areas. While, in the future, it may be possible to test changes in these areas by reference to psycholinguistic tests which have been carried out since the 1960s, we have no corresponding tests carried out in the early years of this century to act as a base of comparison. For a simple example of the type of test meant, see Johansson (1979).

The question of *between you and I* instead of *between you and me* is an interesting one from the point of view of syntactic change. *Between you and I* has long been a non-standard form of English, and it is being heard more and more in otherwise standard contexts. Several of my colleagues use it consistently, even in lectures or in addressing formal university gatherings, for example. The change is the degree to which this construction is now accepted as being a formal one, or the degree to which this is now viewed as standard English. Variability in pronoun usage is actually more widespread than this single example shows. Consider, for example

The news was broken to him by Dexter's phone call to him at Leicester's Grace Road where . . . fate had thrown Gooch and he together in opposition.

(the *Daily Mail*, 9 September 1989, p. 48, col. 3)

We shall find whomever is responsible for this outrage.

(the *Daily Mail*, 23 September 1989, p. 2, col. 1)

There are also cases where a form ending in *-self* is used to avoid the choice of either form of the pronoun:

We specialized in gypsy styles modelled by myself.

(*ALTB*, p. 198)

Colm at nineteen was eight years older than myself when Kilty died.

(*LUTR*, p. 7)

Note that even the normal meaning of *by myself* as 'on my own' does not prevent the first of these.

One relatively well-explored area of syntactic change is the change from *Mrs Thatcher, the Prime Minister*, to *Prime Minister Margaret Thatcher*. For some discussion, see Bell (1988).

Notes for advanced students

The analysis of concord presented in section 3.3 is a fairly superficial one, and a much more elaborate analysis would be possible and might prove to be rewarding. For example, Corbett (1983) presents an analysis of concord in which he predicts the relative frequencies of singular and plural concord in different categories: verbal concord, pronominal concord, and so on. Nixon (1972) gives figures from *The Times* which support such a distinction. Watson (1979) suggests semantico–pragmatic reasons why some nouns appear to be more open to plural concord than others. Where singular concord is used, there is also concord of gender to consider. It is a curiosity of the *Times* corpus, for example, that *the enemy* is masculine between approximately 1940 and 1945, but neuter outside that period. See also section 5.4 below. Countries provide an interesting case. In British and New Zealand Englishes they tend to be singular when regarded as political entities, but plural when regarded as sports teams. So we tend to read, for instance, *New Zealand is to appeal to the UN* but *New Zealand have beaten the Barbarians 32–6*. Concord with the names of countries which are superficially plural (*The Netherlands, The United States, The West Indies*, and so on) provides an interesting minor study of its own.

Kruisinga and Erades (1911, I, p. 62) say that 'personal collectives' such as *police* 'are always treated as plurals'. This is not supported by my data, and there may be a subsidiary change going on in this area.

The statement of statistical significance for the regression in Figure 3.1 is based on a linear regression; a more sophisticated model does not appear to be necessary given the large amount of variability, and since we are only interpolating. One result of this, however, is that the figures cannot be used to extrapolate to years outside the framework of 1900–85: they only show the trend for those years (and in this type of data). As might be expected just from looking at Figure 3.2, the regression in that case shows no significant trend.

As in other places in this book, the analysis which was used in section 3.4 does not necessarily go deep enough to discover all the factors underlying change, or all the ways in which change is taking place. Studies which have considered factors such as the definiteness of the noun which the relative clause modifies or whether or not the relative clause interrupts the main clause (Romaine, 1982; Kikai et al., 1987; Adamson, 1989; Montgomery, 1989) have made interesting discoveries, and other distinctions could also be relevant.

It is assumed in section 3.4 that the distinction between restrictive and non-restrictive relative clauses is a straight-forward one to make. This is not necessarily the case. First, punctuation for relative clauses became standardized fairly recently (Montgomery, 1989, p. 137) and there is still a lot of variation away from any prescribed standard. Secondly, there are examples where there can be doubt as to which reading is intended. Thirdly, it is not clear to what extent all speakers of English make the distinction: other languages such as Maori do not have such a distinction, and speakers of varieties of New Zealand English which are strongly influenced by Maori appear not to make it either (Winifred Bauer, personal communication). Fourthly, the precise definition of the distinction is difficult, anyway. For discussion of this last point, and illustration of some of the others, see Bache and Jakobsen (1980).

Table 3.9 provides a puzzle in the light of the comment by Johansson and Hofland (1989, p. 3) that American English appears to use *that* relatives more often than British English does. The comment is based on the frequency of the words *that* and *which* in the Brown (American English) and Lancaster-Oslo-Bergen (British English) million-word corpora of written English. Such a distinction does not show up in Table 3.9. Clearly, much more remains to be said about the use of different types of relative in different varieties of English.

Exercises

1. An experiment entirely parallel to the one with the comparative and superlative can be carried out with possessive marking. Has there been a change from *The cat's paw* (with synthetic marking of the possessive) to *The paw of the cat* (with analytic marking of the possessive) or *vice versa*? For some discussion see Barber (1964, pp. 132f) and Potter (1969, pp. 105f). You will need to take care in collecting your data, since both -'s and *of* have other uses than that of showing actual possession. It would be advisable to collect only examples in which a paraphrase with *have* or *possess* or *own* is possible, and to classify them according to whether the possessor is human, animate but not human, or inanimate.

    Is there any evidence of a change from synthetic to analytic in your data? Do you think your results have any implications for Barber's and Potter's contention that there is a change from synthetic to analytic in the marking of comparison?

2.★ Repeat the experiment on concord described in the text, but consulting only the sports pages of some newspaper, and taking particular note of the word *team*. How do your results for that word compare with the results given for *government* above?

3. Consult the sports pages of a British and an American newspaper. Is there a distinctive use of concord with collective nouns in the two sources as suggested by Quirk et al. (1985)? Is there development during the twentieth century in both, only one, or neither of your sources?

4. Compare the use of verbal concord with the use of pronominal concord in some corpus. Can you say anything about the way in which the change is spreading in English? Consult Nixon (1972) before beginning.

5.† If you live somewhere where the local standard variety is not southern Standard British English, you might like to compare the use of concord in collective nouns in your local variety with the use described in the text. Take care to use a corpus of equivalent formality and, if possible, subject matter.

6.† It was pointed out that the trend towards singular concord with collectives in British English cannot be due to American influence. It is a commonplace to find British commentators (though not, one hopes, the linguistically enlightened ones) 'blaming' any development which they consider to be undesirable on American influence. Sometimes they are right about the American influence, sometimes not. (Whether a particular development is desirable or not is more often an aesthetic or social question than a linguistic one.) See how many published comments you can find from British, Australian, New Zealand or South African sources which denigrate alleged Americanisms in this way. Letters to the Editor of prestigious journals are likely to provide the best source of such comments. Can you discover whether the commentators are right or not in attributing a development to the influence of American English? How often are such commentators wrong? In cases where you cannot discover whether there is an American source for a particular development or not, how do the commentators know?

7.   Take a popular newspaper like the *Daily Mirror*, the *Sun* or some local equivalent and see whether there is a pattern in the use of zero relatives and preposition stranding in that, just as there was in *The Times*. Does the paper you have chosen show a similar pattern of variation, but with a larger proportion of informal variants on all occasions?

8.   Consider relative clauses in some type of scientific writing from the beginning of the century and the 1990s. The proceedings of a learned society or a learned periodical might provide suitable material. Is there any evidence of change in relative clauses when the style is held (relatively) constant in this way? The same experiment can be tried with other materials, such as sermons (if these are available in published form), school textbooks or letters to the editor of a newspaper such as *The (Manchester) Guardian*.

CHAPTER 4

Sound change

4.1 Introduction

In this chapter we turn to consider changes in sound. For some of the sections you may need to consult the table of phonetic symbols in the preliminary pages if you are not used to reading transcription. You will not be required to read anything more complicated than you have already met in Chapter 1.

In this chapter, reference will be made to a number of different varieties of English, most of them standard Englishes, but some of them non-standard. The standard pronunciation of English in England is usually referred to as the Received Pronunication of British English, and abbreviated to RP. RP is sometimes misleadingly called 'BBC English' or 'The Queen's English' or even 'Oxford English', although you can now hear many other accents on the BBC, and the kinds of English spoken by the Queen or at the University in Oxford are identifiable sub-types of RP. (The people of the city of Oxford speak very differently.) You cannot tell where in Britain speakers of RP come from by their accent. Although RP is spoken by only a small proportion of people in Britain, it is the best-described accent of British English. The reference accent for the United States is something called 'General American' which is spoken outside the southern states and the Eastern seaboard of the USA. As is the case with British RP, you cannot tell from their accent where speakers of General American come from within this large area.

When you think of sound change, you probably think of cases such as the word *matriarch*, which used to be pronounced /meɪtrɪɑːk/ in RP, and is increasingly pronounced /mætrɪɑːk/. That is, you think of cases where one sound is replaced by a different sound. This is one kind of sound change, but it is not the only kind.

The kind of sound change by which /meɪtrɪɑːk/ becomes /mætrɪɑːk/ is a PHONEMIC sound change: one phoneme or contrastive sound has replaced another. /eɪ/ and /æ/ can be seen to be contrastive because *mate* /meɪt/ and *mat* /mæt/ are different words. Because we are aware of /eɪ/ and /æ/ as distinct sounds, different phonemes, it is relatively easy to hear and become aware of changes of this type. We will consider a case of phonemic sound change in section 4.3.

Harder to hear, but also very important as far as general principles of sound change are concerned, is non-phonemic sound change. In non-phonemic sound change the number of contrastive units remains the same, but the pronunciation of one or more of those units changes. Imagine a speaker of RP or General American saying the words *pit, pet, pat,* and then a speaker of Cockney or Australian English saying the same words. All the speakers will make a difference between these words, so they will all distinguish three vowel phonemes. But the pronunciations of these vowels will not all sound alike. Each speaker will make the distinctions in a different way. In fact, these differences may be so great that, if the words are spoken in isolation, an Australian or Cockney saying *pat* may sound rather like a speaker of RP or General American saying *pet.* These accents vary geographically, but it is also possible for accents to vary through time. The relationship between the same accent many years apart may be just the same as the difference between RP and Australian today: the same number of contrastive units, but different pronunciations of those units. We shall consider an example of this kind in section 4.4.

In this chapter we shall consider phonemic and non-phonemic changes, and the examples will also illustrate changes to stress (suprasegmental change) and changes to segments – both consonants and vowels. The particular changes dealt with also allow us to consider different ways of finding data about sound change.

Q *There is variation in English between the pronunciations* [kɒvəntrɪ] *and* [kʌvəntrɪ] *for* Coventry, *and between pronuncia-*

tions with the tip of the tongue touching the back of the top front teeth and the tip of the tongue extending between the front teeth for the first sound in think. *In each case, if this eventually leads to change, will it be phonemic or non-phonemic change?*

A In the case of *Coventry*, the change will be phonemic, because /ɒ/ and /ʌ/ are contrasting units in words like *cot* and *cut*. In the case of *think*, the change will be non-phonemic, because it makes no difference to the number of contrasts or the place where those contrasting sounds appear.

4.2 Change of stress

The phenomenon of stress in English is a very complex one, both in terms of its phonological patterning and in terms of its phonetic realization. Fortunately, an appreciation of these complexities is not necessary for an understanding of the pattern of change that will be demonstrated in this section. All that is required here is an ability to distinguish between a word like *insight*, which is stressed on the first syllable, and a word like *incite*, which is stressed on the second syllable, and to mark the appropriate syllable as stressed. The difference will be written here, following the conventions of the International Phonetic Association (IPA), as '*insight* versus *in*'*cite*.

Q To make sure you are able to mark stress correctly, write down the words demon, demonic, demonology; refer, referee, reference, *and mark where the stress falls in each of them.*

A I use IPA marking for stress in the following, though you may have used another system. You should be able to read the following accurately:
'demon, de'monic, demo'nology
re'fer, refe'ree, 'reference.

You may, if you wish, treat the data in this section as an exercise, working through the material as it is presented, and looking for the generalizations for yourself. Whether you choose this option or not, consider the stresses on the words in (1) as they are heard in the 1990s.

(1) abdomen
    acumen
    anchovy
    bitumen
    climacteric
    dirigible
    exigency
    formidable
    fragmentary
    hospitable
    inexplicable
    metallurgy
    molybdenum
    nomenclature
    pejorative
    precedence
    quandary
    secretive
    sonorous
    vagary

In many of the words in (1), there has been a change in the position of the stress in the course of this century. In Table 4.1, the stress patterns for these words are given as they appear in the first edition of *The Oxford English Dictionary* (*OED 1*) (1884–1928) or in the first edition of Daniel Jones's *English Pronouncing Dictionary* (*EPD 1*) (1917). (In many cases these two sources agree on the pronunciation, but where they disagree, the more conservative pattern has been used in Table 4.1.) If the stress marked there is compared with the current stress, many differences will be found. Where there are differences, there is almost certainly a general pattern of change, so that stress falls in a regular position after the change. That is, there is a regular pattern, a generalization, about the way in which the stress changes.

You should note that it is likely that some of the words in (1) are, for at least some speakers, still stressed the same way as is shown in Table 4.1. That is, the same change has not necessarily taken place in all of these words for all speakers yet, and most dictionaries list a mixture of old and new pronunciations. That is because linguistic changes do

Table 4.1   Stress patterns for
twenty words (as listed in
OED 1 or *EPD 1*)

ab'domen
a'cumen
an'chovy
bi'tumen
climac'teric
'dirigible
'exigency
'formidable
'fragmentary
'hospitable
in'explicable
'metallurgy
molyb'denum
'nomenclature
'pejorative
pre'cedence
quan'dary
se'cretive
so'norous
va'gary

not simply happen overnight, but are introduced gradually.
Some words change before others. That is what is meant by
the term LEXICAL DIFFUSION. Lexical diffusion does not
imply, of course, that the same words always change first
for every speaker. Rather, at any given stage in the process
of a change, there will be some words which have changed
throughout the community, some which are undergoing
change, and where variable pronunciations can be heard,
and some that have not yet begun to change. Change which
operates by lexical diffusion appears to operate in a speech
community following an S-shaped curve, as shown in
Figure 4.1. This can be interpreted in two ways: in Figure
4.1 the *x* axis represents time, while the *y* axis can be
interpreted as representing either the number of speakers
who have made a change in a particular word or the number
of the potential words which have undergone a particular
change. That is, for any particular word, at first only a few
people make the innovation, then the change takes hold,

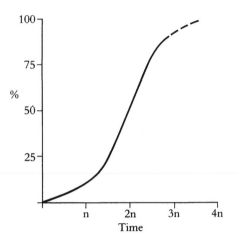

Figure 4.1 S-curve of lexical diffusion. From Chambers and Trudgill (1980, p. 179). The specification of the time periods is their own suggestion.

and people change quite quickly, but the last speakers retaining the old pronunciation change relatively slowly. Alternatively, at first only a few words will change, then more and more will be added relatively rapidly, but the last few words will be slow to make the change.

Q   *If a particular change appears to be affecting only a very few words, what stage of the change process is likely to have been reached?*

A   Either the initial or the final stages; in the middle stage you would expect more words to be affected. However, since the initial and final stages last longer, you are less likely to find a change that is actually taking place at the maximum rate.

Returning now to the words in (1), we can consider the stress patterns they are assigned in late twentieth century reference works, in particular the second edition of the *Oxford English Dictionary* (*OED 2*) (1989), and later editions of Jones's *English Pronouncing Dictionary*. I have consulted the 8th edition (*EPD 8*) (1947), the 11th edition (*EPD 11*) (1956) and the revised 14th edition, revised by Gimson and subsequently by Ramsaran (*EPD 14r*) (1988). In Table 4.2 the more recent (or 'innovative') pronunciation for each of the words given in (1) is provided. An unbracketed source for the pronunciation indicates that the stress marked is given as the most common or only pronunciation for that word in that dictionary; where the source is in parentheses, it indicates that the pronunciation is listed, but not as the most common pronunciation in that dictionary. That is, for those words which only have a parenthesized source next to them, no edition of the *EPD* to date lists the marked pronunciation as the most common one, although it is listed as being found.

The change in every case is a change towards stress on the antepenultimate syllable (the syllable third from the end). This is a change which can be observed taking place in

Table 4.2   Stress patterns for twenty words (as listed in modern reference works)

'abdomen	*EPD 8, OED 2*
'acumen	*EPD 11*
'anchovy	*EPD 11*
'bitumen	*EPD 8*
cli'macteric	*(OED 2)*
di'rigible	*(EPD 8)*
ex'igency	*(EPD 8)*
for'midable	*(EPD 8)*
frag'mentary	*(EPD 1)*
hos'pitable	*EPD 14r*
inex'plicable	*EPD 14r*
me'tallurgy	*(OED 2)*
mo'lybdenum	*EPD 8, OED 2*
no'menclature	*EPD 8*
pe'jorative	*EPD 14r*
'precedence	*EPD 14r*
'quandary	*EPD 11, OED 2*
'secretive	*EPD 14r, OED 2*
'sonorous	*EPD 14r*
'vagary	*EPD 11, OED 2*

English over a long period. *Blasphemous* had the stress on the second syllable at the time of Milton and is still occasionally heard pronounced that way, *character* had stress on the second syllable in the seventeenth century, and *sinister* had stress on the second syllable at the time of Pope. The change from *in'culcate* to *'inculcate* was probably just being completed at the beginning of this century. The modern changes continue this trend. The twenty words listed in (1) are only examples of a much wider pattern. Although the evidence is not always as clear as might be wished, the words listed in (2) all seem to be undergoing (or to have undergone) the same change. In some cases the innovative pronunciation is not yet recorded in the reference books, although it can be heard.

(2)	OLD STRESS	NEW STRESS
	'applicable	ap'plicable
	ar'ticulatory	articu'latory
	Carib'bean	Ca'ribbean
	clan'destine	'clandestine
	con'template	'contemplate
	de'cadent	'decadent
	'despicable	des'picable
	e'querry	'equerry
	eti'quette	'etiquette
	'explicable	ex'plicable
	inde'corous	in'decorous
	in'extricable	inex'tricable
	ir'revocable	irre'vocable
	'lamentable	la'mentable
	'miscellany	mi'scellany
	prema'ture	'premature
	'primarily	pri'marily
	'promissory	pro'missory
	re'condite	'recondite
	re'monstrate	'remonstrate
	re'plica	'replica
	U'lysses	'Ulysses

Despite this very general tendency towards antepenultimate stress in English, there is another observable tendency which sometimes conflicts with the trend to stressing the antepenult. This is a tendency for the base in a morphologically complex word to remain transparent – more easily recognizable. Some suffixes in English regularly cause a change of stress in their bases. Consider the suffix -*ity*. When it is added to the word *fa'miliar*, the stress shifts from the antepenultimate syllable of *familiar* to the last syllable of *familiar* to give *famili'arity*. This change makes the base, *familiar*, less transparent. On the other hand, other affixes such as -*ness* do not regularly affect the stress of the base. *Fa'miliarness* retains a transparent base. Some suffixes, particularly the suffix -*able*, seem to be changing to act like -*ness* although they have previously acted like -*ity* (see further in section 6.2). Some examples are presented in Table 4.3, with old and new pronunciations taken from the same reference works as specified above. Note that in words like *lamentable* and *migratory*, a change to antepenultimate stress also has the effect of making the base more transparent. In these cases the two types of possible change support each other and lead to the same result. Where antepenultimate stress and base transparency conflict, there does not seem to be any way of predicting which tendency will win out. In terms of sheer numbers, antepenultimate stress is the dominant pattern. At the moment, though, I am not aware that forms like those in Table 4.3 are being changed back to antepenultimate stress, so they seem to be stable.

More puzzling than the words listed in Table 4.3 are those words where we can attest a change in stress but where the change is away from antepenultimate stress and

Table 4.3 Stress changes leading to transparent bases

Base form	Old stress	Source	New stress	Source
'capital	ca'pitalist	*EPD 1*	'capitalist	*EPD 8*
con'verse	'conversant	*OED 1*	con'versant	*EPD 11*
'demonstrate	de'monstrable	*OED 1*	'demonstrable	*EPD 1*
'illustrate	il'lustrative	*OED 1*	'illustrative	*EPD 1*
pre'fer	'preferable	*OED 1*	pre'ferable	(*EPD 8*)
sub'side	'subsidence	*EPD 1*	sub'sidence	*EPD 11*
trans'fer	'transference	*OED 1*	trans'ference	(*EPD 8*)

without any compensatory transparency of the base. Words concerned include the following:

(3) OLD STRESS   NEW STRESS
    'doctrinal   doc'trinal
    'expletive   ex'pletive
    'exquisite   ex'quisite
    gla'diolus   gladi'olus
    'jubilee   jubi'lee
    ob'scurantist   obscu'rantist
    'substantive (*adjective*)   sub'stantive (*adjective*)
    'trachea   tra'chea
    'Uranus   U'ranus
    'urinal   u'rinal

All of these have antepenultimate stress listed in reference works for the early part of this century, and all of them have some other stress pattern becoming dominant in the course of the century. In the case of *jubilee* we can perhaps hypothesize that analogy with words such as *amputee*, *nominee* or *dungaree* might cause the change of stress. In the other cases there does not appear to be any particular reason for the change: indeed, in the case of *exquisite*, the new pattern does not even fit general English stress rules. In Gimson (1962, p. 226) it is suggested that this is to give a pattern of alternating relatively stressed and relatively unstressed syllables and to avoid two unstressed syllables next to each other. But this explanation (which would explain some of the changes already shown) does not explain all the changes, even in this final group. Some of these changes also have the effect of destressing a prefix, but not all of the relevant words contain prefixes, so this cannot be the only factor.

In the light of what has been said in this section, we can now consider three words which are frequently held up by purists as examples of the fact that people can no longer pronounce English: *controversy*, *kilometre* and *comparable*. The early twentieth-century pronunciations of these words are '*controversy*, '*kilometre* and '*comparable*. These are now also pronounced with antepenultimate stress, thus: *con'troversy*, *ki'lometre* and *com'parable*. It is not yet clear whether the old or the new pronunciation will prevail. If the pronunciation '*kilometre* is retained, it is a victory for the principle of transparency: both the elements *kilo* and *metre* then retain their pronunciation. But that same principle is likely to lead more and more people to the stress *com'parable*. The stresses that people are complaining about are the natural outcome of a process of change which has been going on for a long time, and which has given us stresses which are accepted unquestioningly today.

4.3 Yod-dropping

You can tell whether or not a word originally contained a /j/ (or 'yod') before /uː/ by the spelling: words with *u(e)* and *ew* used to be pronounced with /juː/, while those containing *oo* and *ou* have always contained /uː/ with no /j/. This was even true in words like *brew* and *blue*. In the sixteenth century, words such as *threw* and *through* were distinguished by the presence versus absence of /j/. However, as can be seen from these examples, not all of these /j/s are retained in current English. Some disappeared as early as the seventeenth century, some are still with us today.

Q *Which of the following words must have contained /juː/ at some stage in their history:* brood, clue, flew, rude, sewer?

A All of them except *brood*.

It will be necessary to consider separately what happens in stressed syllables and what happens in unstressed syllables, since the two are not identical. First consider the current pronunciations of a number of words which contained a yod in the stressed syllable in sixteenth-century English. The current pronunciations are given for three varieties of English: British RP as listed in the revised 14th edition of the *English Pronouncing Dictionary* (*EPD 14r*) (1988), United States English (General American), as listed in the *American Heritage Dictionary* (*AHD*) (1976) and Australian English as listed in the *Macquarie Dictionary* (*MD*) (1981). The pronunciations of the relevant portions of the words are given in Table 4.4. Where Table 4.4 shows alternation, the more common variant is listed first.

The display in Table 4.4 is ordered according to phonetic categories, and the words will be dealt with in the order in which they appear in the Table.

First, *blue* presents the *ue* spelling after a consonant cluster. Here the /j/ has disappeared in all three varieties, although as late as 1944 *A Pronouncing Dictionary of American English* (*PDAE*) was able to list a pronunciation /blɪuː/ as one possible pronunciation of this word for Americans.

Following labial and velar consonants and /h/, the /j/ is retained in all varieties: *beautiful, cute, fume, huge, mute.* The same is true where the /j/ is initial: *ewe.*

After the palatal consonant /ʧ/ the /j/ has gone in all varieties (although the second edition of the *Oxford English Dictionary* has still not removed /ʧjuː/ as a possible pronunciation of *chew*). The same is true after /r/ in *rule*, though again *PDAE* gives /rɪuːl/ as one possible American variant.

This leaves pronunciations where the historical /j/

Table 4.4 Current pronunciations of words with historical yod in three varieties of English

Word	British RP (*EPD 14r*)	US English (*AHD*)	Australian English (*MD*)
blue	bluː	bluː	bluː
beautiful	bjuː	bjuː	bjuː
cute	kjuː	kjuː	kjuː
fume	fjuː	fjuː	fjuː
huge	hjuː	hjuː	hjuː
mute	mjuː	mjuː	mjuː
ewe	juː	juː	juː
chew	ʧuː	ʧuː	ʧuː
rule	ruː	ruː	ruː
enthuse	θuː ~ θjuː*	θuː	θuː ~ θjuː
dew	djuː	duː ~ djuː	djuː
tune	tjuː	tuː ~ tjuː	tjuː
suit	suː ~ sjuː	suː	suː
new	njuː	nuː ~ njuː	njuː
lewd	ljuː ~ luː	luː	luː ~ ljuː

Notes: ~ indicates 'alternates within the community'
* The alternation is shown at *enthusiasm* rather than at *enthuse*

comes after dental and alveolar consonants, and here there are no clear generalizations. We can say that of the three varieties, American English has lost the most /j/s and British RP has retained the most: Australian English represents a middle ground in this respect, although the listings from *MD* make it very close to RP on this parameter.

The variation between /tuː/ and /tjuː/, /duː/and /djuː/, /nuː/ and /njuː/ recorded for US English is perhaps surprising given that Mencken comments in 1936 that 'The schoolmarm still battles valiantly for *dyuty*, but in vain', and goes on to note that pronunciations with /j/ would sound affected in most parts of the US. Certainly it is part of the British image of Americans that they say /tuːn/, /duːti/ and /nuːz/. Wells (1982, p. 247) comments that General American usage is 'not entirely uniform' in this respect, but it seems likely that the variants with /j/ are now used in stressed syllables by only a minority of speakers, even if the /j/ is retained in some southern US areas.

On the basis of the discussion above, we can set up a table which shows the pattern following these consonants more clearly. This is done in Table 4.5, where again the most common member of a pair is listed first in cases of variation.

This produces the following pattern, where the retention of /j/ after a consonant towards the left of the scale implies the retention of /j/ after all consonants to the right of that point, but not vice versa. This kind of pattern,

Table 4.5 Patterns of yod–deletion following dental and alveolar consonants

Consonant	US	AUS	RP
s	∅	∅	∅ ~ j
θ	∅	∅ ~ j	∅ ~ j
l	∅	∅ ~ j	j ~ ∅
n	∅ ~ j	j	j
d	∅ ~ j	j	j
t	∅ ~ j	j	j

where the value for one point in the scale implies values for other points is called an IMPLICATIONAL SCALE.

$$(4) \quad s > \theta > 1 > \begin{cases} n \\ d \\ t \end{cases}$$

This pattern is clearly not the only logically possible one, and we would not necessarily expect other varieties to follow the same implicational scale. Surprisingly, many for which information is available do. Some of the words listed in Table 4.4 were words used in the Survey of English Dialects (SED). The SED was a survey of rural English dialects, carried out mainly during the 1950s, in which dialectal words, grammar and pronunciations were noted. The patterns given by the informants in four of the SED locations in which yod is neither uniformly kept nor uniformly lost are given in Table 4.6. The four locations concerned are Great Dalby, Leicestershire (SED 13/6), Ludham, Norfolk (SED 21/6), Netheravon, Wiltshire (SED 32/6), and Kingston, Dorset (SED 38/5). The information on which this is based can be found in Kolb et al. (1979) and Orton et al. (1978).

In all the dialects illustrated, /j/ has disappeared following a palatal consonant and following a consonant cluster. In the Leicestershire dialect all the other /j/s remain. In the Norfolk dialect the /j/ has disappeared following every consonant except /t/ (although some palatal quality remains in the frontness of some of the vowels: [ʉ] is a

Table 4.6 English–dialect pronunciations of selected words with historical yod

Word	Leicestershire	Norfolk	Wiltshire	Dorset
blue	blʉː	bləʊ	bluː	bluː
chew	ʧʉː	ʧaː	ʧuː	ʧuː
dew	djʉː	dʉː	ʤuː	djuː
ewe	jʉː	jʉː	juː	joː
new	niuː	nuː	niuː	niuː
suit	siuː	sʉː	siuː	suː
tune	tjʉː	tjʉː	ʧuː	ʧuː

fronter vowel than [u]). In the Wiltshire dialect all the other /j/s remain, but they COALESCE with the /t/ and the /d/ to form affricates. In the Dorset dialect the /j/ following the /s/ has gone, but the others remain. While this is clearly not the full possible range of dialect types, these do tend to support the general finding that /j/ is more stable following alveolar stops (/t/ and /d/) than elsewhere following alveolars. This is further supported by the following generalizations based on Kolb et al. (1979) and Orton et al. (1978): no English dialect has /sjuːt/ but /tuːn/; those dialects which pronounce *dew* as /duː/ tend to be a subset of those dialects which pronounce *tune* as /tuːn/; the same relationship tends to hold between pronunciations of *new* and *tune*. There are small enclaves in northern Yorkshire and on the Yorkshire/Lancashire border which have /nuː/ but /sjuːt/, spoiling an otherwise good subset relationship there as well.

If the evidence from these English dialects is taken as equivalent to the evidence from the standard varieties, it seems that it provides evidence for extending the implicational scale in (4) to

(5) $\quad s > \theta > l > \left\{ \begin{matrix} n \\ d \end{matrix} \right\} > t$

It certainly makes it seem that varieties of English that lose /j/ after /t/ and /d/ but retain it after /s/ are, if they exist at all, extremely rare.

Q *What kinds of predictions would you make about likely pronunciations of words like* suited *and* enthusiasm *on the basis of the implicational scale in (5)? What would make you want to change or reject the scale?*

A You would predict that while there may be speakers of some varieties who say /suːtɪd/ for *suited* and /enθjuːziːæzm/ for *enthusiasm*, there will be none that say /sjuːtɪd/ but /enθuːziːæzm/. Similarly for every pair in the scale. Evidence that some speakers said, for example, /ljuːsɪd/ for *lucid* but /tuːtə/ for *tutor*, counter to these predictions, would invalidate (at least part of) the scale.

Now let us consider what happens in unstressed syllables. The pattern when the syllable containing the potential /juː/ is separated from the main stress in the word by an unstressed syllable is just the same as that shown in Table 4.4 above. That is, the patterns of yod-dropping in words like *attitude*, *numismatic* and *lucubration* are the same as those illustrated above. This is probably due to the fact that such syllables receive a certain amount of stress due to their position. The pattern of yod-dropping in syllables adjacent to the main stress, however, is different. This is shown in Table 4.7.

Perhaps the most striking thing about the data in Table 4.7 is the amount of vowel reduction that is shown there. The reduction is most often to /ʊ/ in British RP, much more frequently to /ə/ in US and Australian English. It is also striking that coalescence or merger of /tj/, /dj/ to /tʃ/ and /dʒ/ respectively is much more common in unstressed syllables than stressed ones. This coalescence even extends to /sj/ and (not illustrated because of its rarity) /zj/, giving /ʃ/ and /ʒ/ respectively. This raises the question of whether such coalescence is to be classified as yod-retention or yod-dropping. Such evidence as there is suggests that it must 'count as' yod-retention. First, the palatality associated with the /j/ is retained phonetically in the merged forms: /tʃ/, /dʒ/,

Table 4.7 Patterns of yod-deletion following alveolar consonant in unstressed syllables

Cons	Examples	US (*AHD*)	AUS (*MD*)	RP (*EPD 14r*)
r	'erudite, eru'dition	rjʊ ~ rʊ	rə	r(j)uː ~ r(j)ʊ
s	pe'ninsula	sjə ~ sə	ʃə	sjʊ ~ ʃʊ
s	sensu'ality	ʃʊ	ʃuː	sjʊ ~ ʃʊ
l	'valuable	ljuː ~ ljə	ljuː	ljʊ
l	solu'bility	ljə	ljə	ljʊ
n	'annual, continu'ality	njuː	njuː	njʊ
d	re'sidual, individu'ality	dʒuː	dʒuː	djʊ ~ dʒʊ
t	'statue, punctu'ality	tʃuː	tʃuː	tʃʊ ~ tjʊ

/ʃ/ and /ʒ/ all have (partly) palatal articulation throughout. Secondly, from a phonological point of view affrication of [t] to [tʃ] is generally taken to be a FORTITION or strengthening process rather than a LENITION or weakening (Sommerstein, 1977, p. 228), yet dropping anything is the absolute form of weakening. This implies that yod-dropping and coalescence have opposite effects, not the same effect. Thirdly, it seems in Table 4.6 that the coalesced forms generally co-occur with retained yod, not with dropped yod. If we thus include coalescence under the general heading of yod retention, then yod is retained far more in unstressed syllables than in stressed syllables. The general principle is that it is lost most after /r/ and /s/, but retained elsewhere.

We are now in a position to look at the overall pattern of yod-dropping in English. There seems to be a general pattern that /j/ is less stable following /r/, /s/, /θ/ and /l/ than it is following /n/, /d/ and /t/. The yod coalesces with a preceding /t/ or /d/, especially in an unstressed syllable, to give /tʃ/ or /dʒ/. While the data presented above for standard varieties shows this coalescence occurring only in unstressed syllables it is noteworthy that Horvath (1985) reports coalescence as common in stressed syllables as well in Australian English, and the same is true in New Zealand English. The same general pattern is illustrated by the comment in Orkin (1971, p. 137) that while /juː/ is the overtly prestigious pronunciation in Canada after /t/, /d/ and /n/, it is not much used after /s/ and /l/.

There is, of course, no *a priori* reason why a change that has taken place in one variety of English should be expected to take place in another. Indeed, languages diverge from a single mother language precisely because not all varieties undergo the same changes. Nevertheless, we appear to have here a fairly consistent pattern applying across a number of varieties, and applying in both stressed and unstressed syllables to different degrees. It is thus extremely tempting to make predictions such as that British RP is likely to lose yod in stressed syllables following /s/, /θ/ and /l/ before it loses it following /n/, /d/ and /t/.

There is some evidence that this change is already taking place. One of the few differences in pronunciation of potential yod-words between the first and second editions of the *Oxford English Dictionary* is that *super-* is given the pronunciation /s(j)uːpə/ in *OED 1* but /suːpə/ in *OED 2*. Although /əˈljuːd/ is given as the most common pronunciation of *allude* in the first edition of the *English Pronouncing Dictionary* (*EPD 1*) (1917), in editions published since the middle of the century /əˈluːd/ is the most common pronunciation. In *EPD 14r* the most common pronunciation of *suit* is given as /suːt/, though in *EPD 11* the most common pronunciation was still /sjuːt/. In these reference works there is no change to the pronunciation of words like *new, nude, dew, due, tune, Tuesday* recorded for this century.

In this section we have concentrated on the question of /j/ following dental and alveolar consonants. There is also a problem about earlier yod following other consonants. Some varieties of English, notably East Anglian dialects, drop the /j/ after all consonants (Wells, 1982, p. 207), so that *beauty* and *booty, cute* and *coot* become homophones (though see Kelly and Local, 1989, pp. 139–40 for a different view of this phenomenon). The general assumption is that standard varieties retain /j/ after labials and velars, but this is not always true. The word *recuperate* has lost its /j/ for most speakers in the course of this century (I owe this observation to J. Windsor Lewis). *Figure* retains a /j/ in American, but not in British English. In unstressed position in the word *consecutive* there is frequently no /j/ in New Zealand English. Words like *beautiful* are sometimes heard without a /j/ (or seen spelt *bootiful*) but this is only a jocular pronunciation at the moment, or baby talk. It is too soon to say whether /j/ is likely to be lost before velars earlier than it is lost before labials, or whether the two are likely to go hand-in-hand (assuming, of course, that /j/ is ever lost in these positions).

4.4 Vowel change

In this section non-phonemic change (as introduced in section 4.1) will be illustrated from RP using just three vowels: the vowels /æ/, /ʌ/ and /uː/, as in *sad, sud* and *sued* respectively.

The discussion in this section depends upon an

understanding of how vowel sounds are described. If you already know about this, you can skip the next three paragraphs.

Different vowels are produced by changing the position of the tongue in the mouth and the position of the lips. We will not need to worry particularly about lip position in what follows, but you will be able to feel a difference in lip position (or see it if you watch yourself in a mirror) if you say *pet, port*. You can feel the difference in tongue position if you say *pet, pat, putt*. Along with the change in tongue position, you may find your jaw opening more as you say these three, but if you bite on something like a pencil you will find you can say all three without moving the jaw, and simply by moving the tongue.

Now, although you can feel the tongue move, it is difficult to tell precisely what your tongue is doing in your mouth. Roughly speaking, we can say that it is changing the point at which the space between the upper jaw and the lower jaw (with the tongue attached) is narrowest. But the space in which it is possible to create a vowel sound by movement of the tongue is restricted. If the tongue gets too close to the roof of the mouth, a consonant rather than a vowel is created; on the other hand the tongue is prevented from moving too far from the roof of the mouth by the lower jaw. The area inside which the tongue can move and still create a vowel is called the vowel area. In linguistics textbooks, you will usually find this area presented in an idealized shape, as in Figure 4.2.

Vowel sounds produced with narrowest constriction at the front of the vowel area are called front vowels, those with the narrowest constriction at the back of the vowel area are called back vowels, and those with the narrowest constriction half-way between the two extremes are called central vowels. Vowels produced with the tongue close to the roof of the mouth are called close vowels (or, equivalently, high vowels); those produced with the tongue a long way from the roof of the mouth are called open (or, equivalently, low) vowels. When the quality of the vowels changes over time, we can talk of the vowels raising, lowering, advancing, retracting or becoming centralized in this vowel space.

Much of the evidence we have for the position of vowels in the vowel space is acoustic evidence, based on

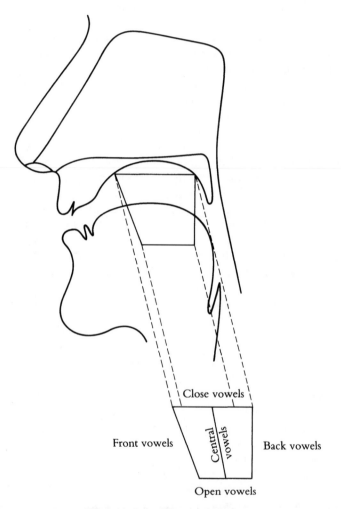

Figure 4.2   The vowel area

spectrographic analysis of the vowels in question and making reference to FORMANT STRUCTURE. An explanation of the term 'formant' is thus required.

Any vibrating sound-source, whether it is a violin string or the vocal folds, produces not only a tone corresponding to the basic speed of the vibration of the source but also a number of harmonics of that tone.

Harmonics are tones with speeds of vibration which are multiples of the speed of vibration of the source. So a violin string playing an A at 440 cycles per second (cps) (that is, the string is vibrating backwards and forwards 440 times every second) will produce harmonics at frequencies of 880 cps, 1320 cps, 1760 cps and so on. A male speaker whose basic pitch is 120 cps will produce harmonics at 240 cps, 360 cps, 480 cps and so on. However, not all of these harmonics reach the ear. The body of the violin on the one hand or the vocal tract (oral, nasal and pharyngeal cavities) on the other have the effect of filtering out some of these harmonics while amplifying others. It is for this reason that an A with a fundamental frequency of 440 cps sounds different when played on a violin and a flute: the different instruments filter out and reinforce different harmonics. In the case of vowel sounds, the result of this process of filtering and amplification is that there are bands of acoustic energy present at different frequencies, and these bands of energy are called formants. Formants can be made visible if the sound is analysed on a sound spectrograph (or more recently by computer programs which do the same job). This equipment produces a print-out, called a spectrogram, with frequency in cycles per second on the vertical axis and time on the horizontal axis. The intensity of the sound at any particular frequency is shown by the blackness of the trace or 'picture'. A spectrogram of the author's pronunciation of the word *fizz* is shown in Figure 4.3. The formants in the vowel section of the word have been marked, numbering them from the lowest frequency formant upwards, as is customary.

For most linguistic purposes, it is the frequencies of the first two formants which are important, higher formants giving the hearer information about the individual speaker rather than about the particular vowel being uttered. The frequency of Formant 1 (F1) gives information about vowel height: the higher the frequency of F1, the more open the vowel is. Formant 2 (F2) gives information about frontness and backness: the higher the frequency of F2, the fronter the vowel is. Thus different formant frequencies correspond to different vowel qualities. If a graph is drawn of the frequency of F1 against the frequency of F2 minus F1 (F2-F1), a very good approximation to the traditional vowel chart can be obtained (see Ladefoged, 1975, for example).

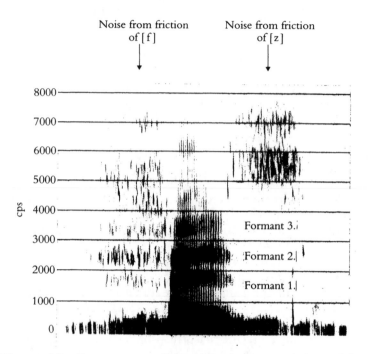

Figure 4.3   Spectrogram of the author's pronunciation of *fizz*,
[fɪzʐ]

Although we shall not need to draw complete vowel charts
in this way, we shall use the general principle below. Where
graphs are drawn of F1 against (F2-F1), then the directions
on the chart correspond to directions within the vowel space
chart given in Figure 4.2. We shall not be concerned with
precise locations in the vowel area, only directions of
change, so we do not need to worry about how precisely
the vowel chart fits the formant figures.

Wells (1962) reports on an experiment in which 25 male
speakers of RP, 23 of them of university age, were asked to
read sentences of the form 'The word is –' into a tape-
recorder. Different words were introduced into the slot, but
all had the consonants /h/ and /d/ surrounding a vowel.
The three in which we are interested here were *had*, *hud* and
who'd. Each sentence was read twice. The vowels were then
analysed on a spectrograph and the average values of the
formants for each vowel were calculated.

Henton (1983) reports on what happened when she repeated the experiment twenty years later. She used 10 male speakers of RP, aged between 25 and 37, and again each read each sentence twice. The spectrographic analysis was carried out using more up-to-date technology, but the principles were still the same. The values of F1, F2 and (F2-F1) for Wells's and Henton's experiments are presented in Table 4.8. The data is presented in diagrammatic form in Figure 4.4.

Table 4.8   Formant frequencies for three vowels of RP measured twenty years apart (male speakers)

	Values for 1962			Values for 1982		
	F1	F2	F2-F1	F1	F2	F2-F1
æ	748	1746	998	713	1615	902
ʌ	722	1236	514	645	1200	555
uː	309	939	630	347	1149	802

Sources: Wells (1962) and Henton (1983)

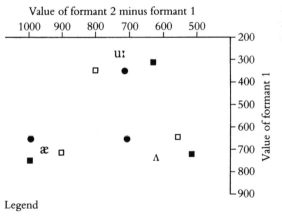

Value of formant 2 minus formant 1

Legend

■ Wells (1962)   □ Henton (1983)   ● Bauer (1985)

Figure 4.4   Diagrammatic representation of vowel change in RP. Data from Wells (1962), Henton (1983) and Bauer (1985)

Q *How will linguistic change show up on the chart? Can you suggest anything about the reliability of such measures?*

A   Linguistic change will show up as a different position on the chart. Because each position is an average of averages, and for only 25 speakers in the one case, 10 in the other, very small differences in position on the chart are unlikely to indicate real change: consistent or patterned changes on the chart are more likely to be meaningful.

The differences between Wells's figures and Henton's figures seem largely to be the result of diachronic change. The change shown here is perhaps not dramatic, but it represents change only over a twenty-year period. We might speculate that changes over a longer portion of the century would be greater. A more marked change, in these and in other vowels, would also account for the common observation that actors in films from the 1930s and 1940s at times sound very strange to our ears today.

In Bauer (1985) I reported on a similar experiment to measure change in RP over a longer period. This experiment was based on recordings made at the University of Edinburgh between 1949 and 1966 of students and staff members reading the story of Arthur the Rat. The version of this story used from 1958 onwards is published in Abercrombie (1964). These recordings, which were made on 78 rpm discs, included versions made by 37 speakers of RP, 18 males and 19 females. Information on the year of birth of these informants was also available. I was also able to obtain tape-recordings of the same text made by students at University College London in 1982. These students were all born much more recently than the speakers in the Edinburgh data. Five female RP speakers from this corpus (there were no relevant male speakers) were added to the Edinburgh corpus. Information on the year of birth of these informants was not available, but they must have been born around or just after 1960. I made a spectrographic analysis of the vowels being considered here using computer software, and calculated average formant frequencies for each speaker. For comparison with Wells's and Henton's figures given above, the average formant values for males from this experiment is recorded in Table 4.9, and was also

Table 4.9 Average formant figures for male RP speakers for three vowels

	F1	F2	F2-F1
æ	652	1647	995
ʌ	658	1365	707
uː	351	1066	715

Source: Bauer (1985)

plotted in Figure 4.4. Since the males whose speech is represented in this Table were born at different times during the century, the figures here cannot be used alongside those of Wells and Henton to illustrate a pattern of change, but they may indicate some kind of average position for the century.

The values for F1, F2 and (F2-F1) for five reasonably representative female subjects are presented in Table 4.10 and plotted in Figure 4.5. The same speakers are used for all three vowels. The speakers chosen indicate how the vowels of speakers born at different times during the century pattern. They are all fairly representative of speakers born at approximately the same time.

In Table 4.10 and Figure 4.5, the values for /æ/ show a retraction and, possibly, a lowering of this vowel over the century. (Retraction is shown in Figure 4.5 by movement to the right, lowering is indicated by movement down the graph.) The lowering effect has been exaggerated by choosing only a small number of the informants, but the retraction comes through clearly even with a larger number of informants. The later in the century an RP speaker was born, other things being equal, the more retracted a variant of /æ/ he or she is likely to have.

The values for /ʌ/ appear to show a general fronting of this vowel, except with the youngest speaker (where the data is not particularly reliable anyway see Bauer 1985, p. 78). Again, the effect is not as clear as this when more informants are considered. We shall see, however, that this trend may be an accurate reflection of change during this century.

The values for /uː/ show a marked fronting of the

Table 4.10 Formant frequencies for five
female speakers of RP from throughout the
century

Speaker	YOB*	F1	F2	F2-F1
/æ/				
1	1919	783	1791	1008
2	1935	706	1643	937
3	1944	779	1726	947
4	1947	936	1732	796
5	ca. 1960	881	1595	714
/ʌ/				
1	1919	786	1378	592
2	1935	644	1409	765
3	1944	796	1634	838
4	1947	688	1574	886
5	ca. 1960	786	1526	740
/uː/				
1	1919	396	996	600
2	1935	388	1097	709
3	1944	398	1384	986
4	1947	391	1557	1166
5	ca. 1960	393	1636	1243

Note: * 'year of birth'
Source: Abstracted from Bauer (1985)

vowel in the course of the century. This trend remains clear
for both male and female speakers even when all the
informants are considered. This fronting of /uː/ is probably
one of the most dramatic changes in the pronunciation of
RP in the latter part of this century, and this particular
methodology allows the change to be seen particularly clearly.

From this material from Bauer (1985), it can be seen
that trends are indeed clearer when a longer period is
considered, and also when individuals are considered, rather
than averages taken over individuals. We now have

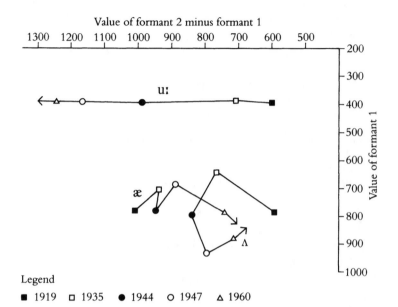

Figure 4.5 Diagrammatic representation of vowel change in RP. Female speakers with different years of birth. Data from Bauer (1985)

recordings going far enough back to make this method of tracing phonetic change perfectly possible – if still extremely time-consuming. If data can be retrieved from broadcasting archives, this kind of work ought to become a very reliable way of tracing phonetic change. It is, in effect, the method that Hockett (1958, p. 439) thought to be impractical (see the discussion above in section 1.2).

Note, however, that not all of the results from my paper agree with the results obtained by Henton (1983) in her comparison with the work of Wells. While Henton and I both agree that /uː/ is being fronted, Henton finds that /æ/ and /ʌ/ are being raised. Henton and I both agree on the retraction of /æ/ but I find no evidence that /æ/ is being raised (indeed, the full set of data suggests that it is being lowered), and have no real evidence for a raising or lowering of /ʌ/. The differences appear to arise from the fact that Henton provides averages over ten speakers, while in my paper speakers are listed individually. The differences do not result from the fact that Henton's informants are male, while those of mine cited here are female: the male speakers in Bauer (1985) show similar trends to the females. If there are other reasons for the differences, it is not clear what they are.

Where such dramatic changes are taking place in the pronunciation of a prestige dialect like RP, it might be expected that these changes would be reflected in the phonetic descriptions of RP given in handbooks published at different times in the course of the century. This is true. These descriptions are given in terms of the Cardinal Vowels. The Cardinal Vowels are a system of standard reference vowels located on the periphery of the vowel area. The positions of the eight primary Cardinal Vowels, as determined by Daniel Jones, are marked in Figure 4.6 on a standard vowel chart, which represents the vowel space.

Ward (1929, p. 67) gives the pronunciation of /æ/ as being a raised Cardinal 4, while Gimson (1962, p. 100) says that it is 'just below half-open [i.e. open-mid] position' and that in 'refined RP' it may be realized as close as Cardinal 3. Thus, in the early part of the century, it appeared that /æ/ was becoming a closer vowel. Later, however, it started to open again, and Wells (1982, p. 292) comments that 'it may even be the case that /æ/ and /ʌ/ are merged, variably at least'. This tendency to opening is commented upon briefly by Gimson (1970, p. 104), but does not appear to be seen as an important trend there.

Jones (1909, p. 41) and Ward (1929, p. 89) describe /ʌ/ as a centralized back unrounded open-mid vowel (which explains why the symbol /ʌ/ is used for this vowel). Gimson (1962, p. 102), on the other hand, describes it as a 'centralized and slightly raised' Cardinal 4. That difference reflects an important degree of fronting in the course of the century.

The phoneme /uː/ is described for most of this century as being a slightly centralized Cardinal 8, but both Gimson (1962, p. 114) and Wells (1982, p. 294) comment on the increasing 'centralization' of /uː/.

These various descriptions are summarized in Figure 4.6.

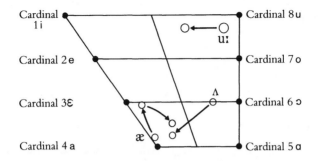

Figure 4.6 Change in selected vowels of RP. Data abstracted from various handbooks (see text)

The handbooks, then, show changes in the same direction as the changes shown in the experiment in Bauer (1985) described above, except that the experimental results found no trace of the early raising of /æ/. This may be because the recordings on which the results are based were all made in 1949 or later. In general, the results from Bauer (1985) show these changes as being far more advanced than the handbooks suggest, and lead to the conclusion that 'In areas where change is on-going, descriptions of RP in the handbooks appear to be about a generation out of date before they are published' (Bauer, 1985, p. 80). This means that however reliable the handbooks may be as a guide to changes which have taken place in RP, they tend to report on changes which are already well-established, not on current changes. For information on current changes, nothing can replace the analysis of actual spoken material.

4.5 Methodological observations

In this chapter, three distinct sound changes in twentieth-century standard Englishes have been considered: stress changes which seem to affect all standard varieties to some extent, yod-dropping, with particular reference to changes occurring in RP, and vowel quality changes in RP. The last of these is purely a phonetic change, the others are phonological. Different methodologies were used in the three cases. To study stress changes, standard reference works published at different times during the century were consulted. To study yod-dropping, a comparative approach based on the study of a number of varieties of English was used, and again backed up with the study of descriptions of RP published at different times during the century. To study the vowel quality changes, instrumental phonetic techniques were used, backed up with reference to hand-books published at various times during the century.

Basically, there are two underlying methodologies available when we are studying language change in contemporary language. The first of these, illustrated here with the study of vowel quality changes in RP, is to consider the raw data and analyse it in an appropriate way. This is, of course, the first century in which it has been even remotely possible to do this for sound change. For changes occurring before about the sixteenth century it is necessary to consult not pronunciations but spellings, and make the further assumption that spellings reflect pronunciations accurately. A certain amount of evidence may also be available from rhymes, puns, and so on. The second way of studying change is to consider not the actual raw data but analyses of that raw data. The analyses may be of different kinds: in this chapter we have used dictionaries and descriptions provided by phoneticians. In some cases the comments of educationalists on the ways in which pupils' language needs to be modified or comments in the press from purists of various descriptions can provide information of this kind. Discussions of the way English changed between the sixteenth and twentieth centuries are often based on the comments of people with educational aims.

Throughout this book, these two basic methodologies have been used over and over again, and which one is chosen depends on the nature of the change being considered. Except in this chapter, we have been concerned with the analysis of written rather than spoken language. There are good reasons for this. The descriptions of English available tend, until very recently, to be based on written rather than spoken usage; this is clearly related to the fact that written texts for analysis are relatively readily available, whereas representative spoken material is not. This is not to say that it is not possible to get hold of taped material of various kinds of English, but simply that such material is not easily available in the same way that written material is available. Basing descriptions on the written form of the language is also related to the fact that it is the written form of the language which is viewed as carrying prestige, and thus being worthy of description. It may also be due to the fact that more people can write standard English than speak with a standard accent, so that a larger percentage of the population produces standard written texts than standard spoken texts. The point about ease of availability of representative texts remains a problem today. Although more and more linguists are becoming interested in the analysis of spoken rather than written language, it is still difficult to get transcriptions of spoken material even from the 1980s. Tapes of spoken language from earlier in the century tend to be of formal spoken English, not informal. Very often this involves the reading aloud of what are basically written texts, so that the special features of spoken language are not present. Even where genuine spoken discourse is involved, the formality is a problem. On the whole, the more formal varieties of English are modelled on written language: they attempt to copy the syntax, the vocabulary and the general style of written language. This is not meant to imply that even formal spoken English is identical to written English, because very few people can really 'talk like a book' without rehearsal. Nevertheless, formal spoken English is, by its very nature, more like written English than colloquial English would be. Thus it seems likely that even if vast resources were invested in providing transcriptions of spoken texts from earlier in the century, the only area of language they would tell us about which was not already known through written language would be pronunciation in formal styles. This means that there are vast areas of potential change which remain undescribed and undescribable. Did people compliment, insult and apologize to each other in the same way in 1900 as they do in 1990? The only evidence is indirect – through plays and the like, which are not necessarily accurate reflections of the way in which speakers actually behave. Thus even today, methodological considerations control the aspects of language change which we can study with any hope of success. This point, too, will also apply to the changes described in Chapter 5.

Reading and References

4.2   Change of stress

Comments on changes to stress patterns can be found in Burchfield (1981), Gimson (1962, pp. 226–7, or later editions, see 'Word Pattern Instability'), Ladefoged (1975, p. 108), Potter (1969, p. 24) and Strang (1970, pp. 53–6). Lass (1987a, pp. 113–4) provides a simple version of the general English stress rules, which can be developed with reference to Fudge (1984) or Kingdon (1958). For details of the phonetic structure of phonological stress, see Fudge (1984, pp. 1–3) or Gimson (1962, ch. 9), though he uses a different terminology.

4.3   Yod-dropping

The label 'yod-dropping' comes from Wells (1982), where the subject is treated fairly thoroughly. Changes in this area in twentieth century English are mentioned briefly by Barber (1964, pp. 43–4), Gimson/Ramsaran (1989, p. 214) and Potter (1969, p. 20). Horvath (1985) considers the situation in Australian English.

Bailey (1977) provides a hierarchy of positions of yod-dropping which is in the same spirit as the one presented here, though the details of the hierarchies differ.

4.4   Vowel change

For a fuller introduction to the formant structure of vowels, see Chapter 8 of Ladefoged (1975) or a specialist work on acoustic phonetics, such as Fry (1979).

The female speakers cited from the study in Bauer (1985) are the speakers there referred to as 1956, 6506, 6736 and 6849. The data for the speaker recorded in 1982 is the first of the speakers listed in Bauer (1985), though it should be noted that the value for /ʌ/ is an average over all five speakers, not the value for a single individual.

As well as the studies cited in the section, Bauer (1979) presents an attempt to trace phonetic change in twentieth-century RP by a study of the published descriptions. An attempt is also made there to provide a systematization of the general picture of change.

General

For general changes in RP pronunciation see Gimson (1964), Burchfield (1981), and Ramsaran (1990).

Notes

4.2 Change of stress

In some cases, dialects may differ in the way in which they stress the words under consideration here. For example, the *CDE* suggests that *metallurgy*, *miscellany* and *nomenclature* are stressed differently in British and American English. If this is correct, note that American English retains the older pronunciation. This is just one way in which American English is more conservative than British English in pronunciation, though it is frequently more innovative in other ways.

Other changes in suprasegmental phonology occurring in standard Englishes during the twentieth century include the increase in the use of the high rise terminal (also sometimes called Australian Question Intonation) in Australian and New Zealand English, and increasingly also in American English. This is the intonation pattern that makes Australians and New Zealanders sound to speakers of other varieties as if they are asking questions when they are not. There are also at least sporadic changes in the stresses of two-syllable words such as *research* (noun), *decade*, *adult*.

4.3 Yod-dropping

For those speakers who do not have /j/ after /n/, /d/ and /t/, the generalization that is often made is that yod is dropped following all [+ coronal] consonants, that is, after all consonants that are articulated with the blade of the tongue.

Within the general pattern that has been presented here there are some problem pronunciations. For example it is perfectly standard in New Zealand English to delete yod in the word *nude*, although it is generally retained following /n/. Casual pronunciations of the name *New Zealand* are, however, also frequently heard with no /j/.

Gimson (1962, pp. 209–10) notes that in unstressed syllables uncoalesced versions of /tj/ and /dj/ are 'characteristic of careful speech' in modern RP. This suggests that the coalesced forms are the innovative ones. Wells (1982, p. 248) states that coalesced forms in which /nj/ and /lj/ merge and become palatal can also be heard, giving forms like annual [æɲəl] and failure [feɪʎə].

4.4 Vowel change

Studies of the kind reported on here have been carried out for non-standard varieties of American English by Labov and his colleagues. Hartman (1984) considers possible changes in standard American English, although his material is less systematically collected. Phonetic change is taking place in standard Englishes in the starting position of diphthongs, as well as in the vowels discussed in section 4.4. Wells (1982) discusses the regional variation involved here under the title 'diphthong shift'.

General

Other areas where there may be phonological changes taking place in current standard Englishes include the merger of /ʊə/ and /ɔː/ in words like sure, poor, cure so that sure and shore sound the same, and so do poor and pour. In some varieties this merger is more restricted following a /j/, in other varieties the /j/ does not seem to make any difference. In RP there is also change to the incidence of /ə/ and /ɪ/ in unstressed syllables, with /ə/ becoming more common, and in the use of a close vowel rather than a near-close one in positions such as the final syllable of pity. Both these changes have progressed much further in Australian English. A merger between /ɔː/ and /ɔə/ is reported as taking place in RP during this century, although it is not clear how distinct /ɔə/ has been at any stage during the century. In New Zealand English a distinction between /hw/ and /w/ in pairs like whales and Wales seems to have been gradually disappearing in the course of this century. There is also some slight evidence of increasing rhotacism in New Zealand English; that is, the letter r is being pronounced in words like car and farm, and especially in the name of the letter R. Such pronunciations still seem to be restricted to young speakers. In the name of the letter this phenomenon is not restricted to New Zealand.

In some varieties of American English, a merger is currently taking place between /ɔː/ and /ɑː/ so that *caught* and *cot*, *stalk* and *stock*, *Dawn* and *Don*, *naughty* and *knotty* are becoming indistinguishable. Description of the merger is complicated by various regional differences in the distributions of these vowels, but the merger itself is not regionally limited. For some discussion see Wells (1982, pp. 473–6).

There is a great deal of variation between /s/ and /z/ intervocalically in words like *positive* in many varieties of English, but it is not clear to me whether this indicates a change taking place or not.

Notes for more advanced students

Henton (1983) comments that Wells is often credited with having found formant frequencies very different from those he actually cited in his thesis, which may account for differences in the formant frequencies for RP vowels given here and in other publications. There are surprisingly few independent studies of the acoustic nature of RP vowels; much more is available on the vowels of General American English.

It was commented above that Bauer (1979) attempts a systematization of vowel change in twentieth-century RP. This paper has, however, been severely criticized on a number of grounds by Matthews (1981), and the two papers should be considered together and with the brief elucidation in Bauer (1982).

Generally, discussion of stress in English takes place in the context of how individual words should be stressed given their phonological and morphological make-up. It is noteworthy that where there is a change of stress there is frequently also a change in segmental form, so that stress can still be predicted from the segmental form of the word. Consider /ˈdɒktrɪnəl/ versus /dɒkˈtraɪnəl/, for example, where the heavy penultimate syllable in *doc'trinal* attracts the stress, and where penultimate stress would not be possible with the first segmental form given above. Consideration of the stress rules provided by Chomsky and

Halle (1968) or any more recent up-date within the frameworks of Lexical Phonology or Metrical Phonology, and the way they apply to the forms cited in this section should make this point.

The discussion of transparency of bases could be reformulated in terms of Chomsky and Halle's (1968) notation of + -boundaries and − -boundaries, or in terms of levels as in Lexical Phonology. This theoretical infrastructure is, however, not necessary to an understanding of the basic point, and the data presented here appears to provide mild counter-evidence to the theory of Level Ordering. For an introduction to Lexical Phonology, see Mohanan (1986) or Chapter 5 of Goldsmith (1990).

The question of whether the change [tj] → [ʧ] is a fortition or a lenition is more contentious than I made it appear in the text. Although Sommerstein's position on this matter is a widely accepted one, Lass (1984, p. 178) suggests that affrication is lenition. This just makes the point, already made in Bauer (1988b), that a better definition of lenition is still required. As far as the argument in the text is concerned, if this particular part of it does not hold, then it is to be hoped that the other parts of the argument are sufficient to make the case.

It may be possible to go beyond the discussion in the text, and present evidence on the internal relationships between the members of each of the groups of phonemes /s/, /θ/, /r/ and /l/, on the one hand, and /n/, /d/, /t/ on the other. Yod-dropping after /n/ is more common than after /t/ and /d/ in New Zealand English, but there may be a correlation between those who affricate /tj/ and /dj/ and those who drop /j/ after /n/. A larger scale study would be required to discover whether this is or is not the case, and also to see whether there is any such correlation in other varieties.

Exercises

1.* Make a list of all the words used as examples of (possible) stress change in this chapter, and look them up in three or four dictionaries published after 1980. How much variation is there in the stress patterns given by the dictionaries?

Which words appear to have stable pronunciations? Now ask the members of your class to mark the way in which they would stress these words. Do your informants agree with the dictionaries? Are there any patterns which emerge?

2. There are a number of words where other regional varieties of English do not have the same stress pattern as the standard English of England. If you speak one of these varieties, how many such words can you find from your variety? If you speak a variety close to standard English English, how many words can you find that are stressed differently in standard American English? Is standard English English consistently conservative, consistently innovative, or does it vary? (Some words provide no evidence: *spec'tator* and *dic'tator* are regularly formed from *spec'tate* and *dic'tate* respectively, while *'spectator* and *'dictator* are regularly formed from *'spectate* and *'dictate* respectively, without it being clear from this evidence alone which form is innovative. Nothing has been said in this chapter about two-syllable words.) As well as the words listed in the chapter, and in the notes above, you may like to consider words like *advertisement, aristocrat, Cherokee, corpuscle, dislocate, enquiry, realize, vibratory.*

3.† Consulting the general English stress rules provided by Lass (1987a, pp. 113–14) or Fudge (1984, p. 29), show how changes of segmental pronunciation concomitant with changes of stress keep the stress predictable from the segmental pronunciation (as indicated above in 'Notes for more advanced students'). Do you find any exceptions?

4.† Can you find any changes in the stresses of di-syllabic words in the course of the twentieth century? Is there any pattern to such changes?

5.† Read what Gimson (1962, p. 227, or later editions) has to say about changes in stress providing a pattern of alternating relatively stressed and relatively unstressed syllables (what Lewis, 1969, p. 53 calls 'the natural trochaic rhythm of unhurried English speech', but see Brown, 1977, p. 43 for a contrasting view). To what extent is the move to antepenultimate stress documented in this chapter simply a result of a change in favour of alternating stress? Bear in mind Lass's (1987a, p. 114) 'overriding principle: stress, where possible, should not come more than three syllables from the end [of the word. LB]'.

6.★ Choose any dictionary that has been issued in several editions in the course of the century: *Chambers's Twentieth Century Dictionary* or *The Concise Oxford Dictionary* would be suitable examples although they do not use IPA representations of pronunciation, and you should make sure you can interpret their re-spelling systems. Trace the development of the pronunciation of the words listed in section 4.2 through the various editions of the dictionary. Are the words recorded as changing their pronunciations in the same order in the dictionaries you consult and the ones that were used in writing this section? Can you explain your finding here?

7.† If you have access to equipment for making palatograms, check your own pronunciation of a word like *failure*. Is the lateral alveolar or post-alveolar?

8. Some speakers from North America, Wales and the North-East of England retain /j/ in words like *blue*. If you are a speaker of such a variety, or if you can find a speaker of such a variety to act as an informant, try to ascertain whether there is any yod–deletion, and if so whether it conforms with the general pattern that has been set out in this section.

9.★ Take a number of different descriptions of one standard variety of English, published at different times during the century. Do their descriptions of the positions in which /j/ is pronounced change as the century goes on? If so, do they change in the direction you would now expect?

10. Either record an elderly speaker of a standard variety of English or find a tape of a speaker from earlier in the century. Can you find places where the distribution of /j/ has changed?

11. Choose any monophthong of RP not discussed in this section, and consider twentieth-century descriptions of it. Is there any change recorded? /iː/, /ɪ/, /e/ and /ɔː/ are likely to be the most interesting vowels to consider.

12. If several people in your class have attempted to answer the last question, it may be possible to pose a new one. Is there any observable pattern of changes occurring in the RP monophthongs?

13. Although the resources are not as full for all standard Englishes, it should be possible to carry out exercises (11) and (12) for Australian and General American English. Take the advice of your tutors on works to consult.

14. If we take seriously the notion that the handbooks are always a generation behind the actual facts, we would expect young speakers of standard varieties to have changed further than is shown in the reference works referred to. For either stress or yod-dropping, design an experiment to discover whether or not this is true.

CHAPTER 5

Other changes

5.1 Punctuation and formal aspects of writing

Write down your name and address as though you were
addressing a letter to yourself.

Now that you have done that, look at the way in which
you have written the street name. You have almost certainly
written the street name, then a space and then, starting with
a capital letter, the street type (*Street, Road, Avenue, Crescent*
or whatever). This is a new way of writing the street name,
which has come in during this century. Let us assume that
you live in Wellington Street. If you had had a letter to the
editor published in *The Times* of London on Saturday, 20
August 1932, your address would have appeared as
Wellington-street. If your letter had appeared on Monday,
22 August 1932, your address would have appeared as
Wellington Street. *The Times* made the change with no fuss
or dramatics in a single weekend. It could do that because it
was being conservative. The less conservative *Manchester
Guardian* had made the change in about 1908. The date is
left vague because there was not, in the *Manchester Guardian*,
an abrupt switch to the new system as there was in *The
Times*. In February 1908 it is possible to find editions of the
Manchester Guardian which include examples parallel to
Wellington-street and *Wellington Road*. This shows the
probable origin of the change. *Wellington Street* receives
(still) a single stress, while *Wellington Road* receives two.
This is consistent across most varieties of English. There is
no obvious reason for this distinction. Most street types
behave like *Road* in this respect: they demand a second
stress. There are two stresses on *Wellington Avenue,
Wellington Crescent, Wellington Terrace*. *Street* is the odd one

out. If it became the custom to write those street names with two stresses as two words, then street names that ended in *Street* would have been in a minority, which must have created considerable pressure for change.

This is a change which has no linguistic consequences: the spoken language was precisely the same before and after the change, and there is no change to the system in the written language, only to the form of presentation. It is purely a change in orthography, although incidentally it makes English looks less Germanic and more Romance in the way in which it handles addresses.

Return now to the address you wrote. Did you put a comma at the end of each line of the address or not? Did you put a comma after the house number? One book on letter-writing technique (Smith, 1985, p. 12) notes that 'Nowadays, it is usual not to include punctuation in the address', although most people still seem to use commas when they are writing by hand. Given the increased use of automated letter sorting in the post offices, the use of all punctuation marks is now being officially discouraged. Did you write your address with each line slightly offset, or did you 'block' the address? That is, did you write

(1)   Dr P. Smith,
      29, Wellington Street,
        Johnsonville,
          Wellington.

or did you write

(2)   Dr P. Smith,
      29, Wellington Street,
      Johnsonville,
      Wellington.

The latter is now the more common form in business communication, because of the increase in the use of technology such as the typewriter and the word-processor. Again, this change is not a change in the spoken language, and not a change in the system of the written language, only a change in form of presentation.

The obvious place to look for change in punctuation during this century is in the use (or misuse, some might say) of the apostrophe. There is certainly plenty of variation in the way in which the apostrophe is used, though it might be argued that all such variation is variation away from the standard, and not variation within the standard. Unfortunately, there is plenty of evidence that the rules for the use of the apostrophe, which are of remarkably recent origin in any case, have been breached ever since they were set down (Little, 1986). Evidence for change is much harder to find than evidence of variation. There seems to me to be a sub-regularity developing, whereby the apostrophe is used before a plural -*s* when the stem ends in a vowel other than -*e* (hence forms like *pizza's*, *piano's* as plurals), but evidence for any such change cannot be found in edited and published work, and in any case, even this usage has a venerable ancestry.

Nevertheless, there is one place where the use of the apostrophe can be shown to have changed over the century. One of the major American works on style is *A Manual of Style*, published in Chicago and updated regularly. In the 9th edition of 1927, §216, it is stated that 'The plurals of numerals ..., and of rare or artificial noun coinages, are formed by the aid of an apostrophe and *s*.' By the 12th edition of 1969, §6.5, the prescription has changed to 'so far as it can be done without confusion, single or multiple letters used as words, hyphenated coinages used as nouns and numbers ... form the plural by adding *s* alone.' The place where this is most obvious is in phrases such as *the 1960s*, which used to be written *the 1960's*.

Other punctuation conventions are also changing. I considered a selection of fifteen books published by Longman, Green in the years round 1900, and only one did not consistently put a space before a question mark. In a selection of fifteen books published by the Longman group in the years round 1990, only one did put a space before a question mark.

Although *A Manual of Style* consistently recommends that a comma should be used before a conjunction at the end of a list (so you are told to write *men, women, and children* or *apples, pears, or oranges*, and so on), this system is now used irregularly. In the fifteen books mentioned above published ca. 1900, I noted only one as being inconsistent about this usage; the others included a comma. In the 15 books published ca. 1990, five used a comma consistently, four used no comma consistently, and six were inconsistent. It appears that no comma is more likely when simple nouns are listed (as above) than when clauses are listed. So commas are still used in sentences such as *We should read all these books, digest them at our leisure, and comment on them only after some thought.* Similarly, although *A Manual of Style* recommends the use of a full stop after titles such as *Mr*, noting, in the 1927 edition that 'British practice countenances the omission of an abbreviating period after Mr' (1927, p. 82), the books published ca. 1900 universally used the full stop, while those published ca. 1990 tended not to (one out of fifteen did, but I found no relevant examples in eight). It is, however, a matter of house style for Longman that the full stop should be omitted in such cases, so the figures may not indicate the extent of variation in the community, at either period. Even the fact that house style has apparently changed (as with the space before question marks mentioned above) may be significant in tracing such change, though. The change was probably prompted by changes in other house styles partly as a result of a perception of change in the wider community and possibly partly in an attempt to make the printed page look less cluttered.

5.2 Spelling

There are a few places where people are very aware of spelling variation. In particular, there is known to be variation between *honor* and *honour*, *center* and *centre*, *traveler* and *traveller*, and *characterize* and *characterise*. While there is plenty of evidence of variation here (especially variation determined geographically, so that American writers prefer the first option in each pair listed above, with British or Australasian writers more likely to choose the second option), there is far less evidence of change.

Let us consider the *-ize/-ise* variation, which is not merely a matter of American versus non–American (Oxford dictionaries list *-ize* as the preferred variety, for instance). Of the fifteen books published ca. 1900 mentioned in the last section, seven used *-ize* spellings and eight used *-ise* spellings. In the fifteen books published ca. 1990, eleven used -*ize* spellings and four used -*ise*. The difference is not great enough to indicate anything very clearly, especially in the light of some other information. In the one million words of the Wellington Corpus of Written New Zealand English (Bauer, 1993b), both -*ize* and -*ise* spellings are found, but -*ize* is found largely in technical writing (Bauer, 1993a). The books sampled ca. 1900 dealt largely with history, biography, and theology; the books from ca. 1990 come from a far wider range of subjects, including mathematics, biochemistry and linguistics. These technical works are more likely to be aimed at an international audience, an audience including Americans, and -*ize* may be chosen with this in mind. Perhaps there is a more prosaic reason. Most spelling checkers in word–processing programs will accept only -*ize* or -*ise* spellings, but not both. It is thus easier to adopt the spelling system your spelling checker can cope with. Since most such programs are American in origin, it seems likely that -*ize* spellings predominate in spelling checkers. This reason could, in the longer term, lead to real change in this area.

Q *Can you think of any reasons for preferring* –ise *to* –ize *or vice versa?*

A The most obvious reason is one of frequency, but there are other reasons. You might prefer -*ize* because the sound in the suffix is /z/ not /s/, or because it goes back to a Greek suffix you would want to transliterate with a *z*. You might prefer -*ise* because it allows you to see the relationship with words that end in -*ist* or -*ism*, or because then you do not have to remember that words like *advertise* or *chastise* are never spelt with a *z*. Ostensibly aesthetic reasons, such as 'I think -*ise/-ize* looks better', probably mask some other reason, of which you may not be aware. Typically in language study, such reasons are fronts for social judgements, such as 'I think it is more sophisticated to use -*ise/ -ize*', which can be rephrased as 'I think the people I want to be associated with use -*ise/-ize*'.

There is some slight evidence of change in other areas. While eleven of the fifteen books published ca. 1900 wrote *judgment* and only one used *judgement* (I found no relevant words in the others), by 1990 *judgement* was favoured by ten, *judgment* used by three. In the Corpus of New Zealand English, both occur, *judgement* twenty-nine times, *judgment* twenty-two times (along with *acknowledgement* five times, *acknowledgment* three times, and *fledgling* once). As a rough generalization, the press favours the forms with no *e*, and may be acting as a conservative force here.

Everyone knows that the English spelling system is a nightmare. In fact, the popular view of English spelling as being totally without system severely overstates the case – there is a lot of regularity in English spelling. One estimate is that 84 per cent of English spelling is regular (cited in Crystal, 1987, p. 214). Nevertheless, it is true that there is also a lot of irregularity. Many European nations – the Danish, the Dutch, the Germans, the Norwegians, the Russians, even, recently (though with less success) the French – have official spelling reforms, and change their spellings to fit pronunciations. If English spelling is so bad, why have we not had any English spelling reform? We can divide the answers into a number of different types, including answers based on economics, those based on universality and those based on linguistic principles.

The economic answer is that it would simply cost too much to retrain typesetters, proofreaders, school-teachers and others concerned with the production of the printed word, and to reprint all the necessary books in the new spelling system. This argument may or may not be convincing. If the new system meant that children learned to read and write faster, there might also be economic gains in the new system, although they would not be easy to quantify.

The first answer based on universality relates to the lack of continuity. If English spelling changed, the argument runs, older English texts would become harder to read. Eventually, if spelling reform became a generally accepted principle, more and more changes would be imposed, and it would take special training to read earlier texts, in much the same way as it takes special training to read the Middle English text given in section 1.1.2. While this is obviously true, it is not clear that it matters. Special training is required to read sixteenth-century texts today, because of ways in which the meanings of some words have changed. In another four centuries, special training will be required to read twentieth century texts, too, whether or not there has been spelling reform.

The second answer based on universality relates to geographic universality, and is partly a linguistic argument. It is generally assumed that if there is to be spelling reform, the reform should make the spelling more like the pronunciation of the words. Languages like Finnish and Spanish are held up as ideals in this regard: if you say a word in these languages, you can tell how to spell it; if you see a word spelt, you know how to pronounce it. Where English is concerned, the question immediately arises: whose pronunciation should we base a spelling system on? If we simply base spelling on each individual's pronunciation, we could end up with several hundred million spelling systems. Even if we can define 'standard' in a suitable way, and only have spelling systems for standard varieties, we will have perhaps a dozen different spelling systems. For example, in standard American English *ant* and *aunt* sound the same, as do *plait* and *plate*, but *father* and *farther* are pronounced differently; in RP the opposite is the case. In standard Scottish English, *cot* and *caught* sound the same, as do *pull* and *pool*, but for many speakers *per* and *purr* sound different; in RP the opposite is the case. For many Australians, *chatted* and *chattered* sound the same, and *dance* rhymes with *manse*; for RP speakers, neither of these things is true. If we have different spelling systems reflecting these different pronunciations, and again if spelling reform were to become an established practice, it would in time become harder to read what had been written in another part of the world, and the unity of English, and thus some of its value as a language of international communication, would be lost.

Again, this is true. What is not clear is how much difference it would make. We can – on the whole – understand spoken American or Scottish English, even if we don't come from there. (There are some notable exceptions, but even in these cases, it is possible to understand after a little exposure as long as there is some good will involved.) Would the problem be any greater in the written form? Does unity in writing matter when there is no unity in pronunciation?

A variety of linguistically based reasons for not having spelling reform are generally provided, but as you might expect, not all of these are equally good. First, it is noted that our current spelling system allows us to distinguish in writing between homophones. So while *there* and *their* may sound the same, we can tell which one we mean when we write them down. This reason is not a very strong one. In a sentence like *I saw* /ðeə/ *new car*, the word must be *their*, and in *It was standing just* /ðeə/ the word must be *there*. That is, in context we are unlikely to need the help the spelling provides. Moreover, there are still plenty of homophones which are not distinguished by spelling: *bank* of a river and *bank* for money, *ear* of corn and *ear* for listening, *bear* the animal and *bear* 'to carry', for example.

Some people argue that English spelling encodes etymological information, and that if spelling were changed we would lose information about the origins of words. This, of course, is true: words containing the letter sequence *ph* are all derived from Greek, and, correspondingly, such words tend to occur most often in learned writing. Again, it is less clear whether it would matter if this information were lost. We do not need to know where a word has come from to use it properly; indeed, the idea that a word's current meaning is, or should be, constrained by its etymological meaning is frequently called the 'etymological fallacy' by linguists (see McArthur, 1992). Do you use the word any better if you realize that *darling* is etymologically related to *dear* than if you do not recognize this? In any case, etymological information would not be lost, but simply less superficially obvious.

More importantly, it is pointed out that English spelling has not only phonemic value in that the letters represent the sounds of the words, but also MOR-PHOPHONEMIC value. To understand this, consider the words *sign* and *signify*. The g in *sign* is not pronounced /g/, but in *signify* the g is pronounced /g/. Writing *sign* shows us that the meaning 'sign' is involved both in *sign* and *signify*. If our spelling were based entirely on pronunciation, and we had spellings corresponding to /saɪn/ and /sɪgnɪfaɪ/, this reference to common meaning – to a shared MORPHEME – would be lost. It is this morphophonemic aspect of the English spelling system which leads Chomsky and Halle

(1968, p. 49) to say that the current system comes 'close to being an optimal orthographic system for English'. There might not be many who would agree with this extreme statement, but it is nevertheless the case that this is an important aspect of the English spelling system which is often overlooked by those in favour of reform.

To see how widespread an effect ignoring the morphophonemic aspect of English spelling would have, consider what would happen in NON-RHOTIC varieties of English, that is those where no /r/ is pronounced in words like *farm, corner*. These varieties include RP, standard Australian and New Zealand English, and many of the regional accents of Eastern and Northern England. A word like *farm* would not present any problem in such varieties, because it is always /fɑːm/, and could be spelt to match the pronunciation. But a word like *corner* would provide problems. In isolation, or in a phrase like *the corner she was hiding in* there is no /r/ on the end of *corner*. But when the next word starts with a vowel, as in *the corner of the room, the corner I was hiding in*, an /r/ is pronounced. Moreover, /r/ is pronounced in *cornering* but not in *corners, cornered*. If spelling were purely phonemic, therefore, rather than morphophonemic, we would need two spellings for *corner*, one for *corner she, corner* [pause], *corners, cornered, corner cupboard*, and so on, another for *corner of, corner I, cornering*, and so on. What is more, the same would be true of every English word currently written with a final *r*. The current morphophonemic practice does not seem inefficient or misleading in such instances.

Perhaps the major forces against spelling reform, though, are simple inertia and the conservatism built into any such system. For people who have already learned to read and write (which includes those who would have to introduce new laws, of course) the status quo is easier, there is no need to change spelling systems. Indeed, the pressures are stronger than that. Once you have mastered a system that allows you to spell *cough* and *through*, spellings like *koff* and *throo* just look ignorant, and you are therefore reluctant to adopt them.

Finally, it should be noted that there is no English Academy, as there is a French Académie or Danish Sprognævn to make appropriate recommendations and draft legislation to give them effect. While such institutions frequently act as conservative forces, spelling reform is one area where they can provide a force for change. These days, if anybody tried to set up such a body for the English language, it would presumably have to be an international body. This would in itself make agreement more difficult, given the different varieties of English spoken in different places around the world.

Whether all these reasons for the lack of official spelling reform in English this century add up to a coherent argument, and whether the advantages of the status quo really outweigh the advantages of changing English spelling is a matter of debate. The final nail in the coffin of spelling reform seems to be that people cannot agree about a new system. Without such agreement, no change is likely to occur.

Q *Consider the words* society, social, sociology *and the words* sober, sobriety. *Is there any morphophonemic value in our current spelling system illustrated in these words? How might you spell these words in a revised spelling system?*

A Yes, there is morphophonemic value in the spelling system shown in these words: the sequences *soc* and the *sobr* are found throughout the sets, even though these letters are pronounced differently (you may pronounce the *soc* in *social* and *sociology* the same way or differently).

How these words would be re-spelled is a much harder question, and in fact several problems are raised by the words listed above, including the one of final *r* discussed in the text. Let us consider just two. First, the spelling of the /ʃ/ in *social*. If sound is our major criterion for respelling, then the /ʃ/ in *social* should be spelled the same way as the /ʃ/ in *ship*. Something like *soshal* thus seems called for. Some people have suggested that, since /ʃ/ is a single sound, a single letter should be used, such as *q*, which could be replaced in its current usage by *kw*. Secondly, there is the problem of /ə/ as in the first syllable of *society* or the last of *social*. Not only is it spelled with *a* and *o*, but also with *e* in *kindred*, *i* in *alibi* and with *u* in *suppose*. It is the commonest vowel sound in English, but has no symbol of its own because it is nearly always in morphophonemic variation with some other vowel (eg. in *supposition*) whose letter it adopts. Dealing with /ə/ is one of the major problems faced by any attempt at spelling reform in English.

5.3 Modes of address

How do you address a friend of your parents' (and of their generation) who is not a relation? The following article comes from *The Times* of 2 March 1955, p. 9, col. 4.

Cousin Belinda

Cousin Belinda must be getting an old lady now. Indeed, those who speak of her thus are so elderly themselves that it is highly probable that poor Cousin Belinda is dead. It seems rather sad when some pleasant, old manner of address fades out of fashion. And this one was not only pleasant; it was useful and unembarrassing. It combined family affection with a proper respect for one of your father's or mother's generation, a first cousin once removed. She was rather like a Yorker in the ancient story; what else could you call her? For that matter what does bold faced youth call her in the present incarnation? Sometimes, indeed often, simply her Christian name, but that was once unthinkable; Belinda *tout court* would have represented the height of pertness; sometimes again, and that is certainly much better, she is given the temporary or acting rank of aunt. That may be very proper if she is really worthy of it, but it may imply an unwarranted degree of affection. It also demands a tiresome amount of genealogical explanation. Cousin Belinda, with its pretty touch of formality, filled the bill to perfection.

And apropos of aunts, another old fashion has almost or entirely departed, this time quite unregretted – namely that of calling uncles or aunts by their surnames. The rules have now become very dim.

The custom of calling such a person an aunt or an uncle is first noted in the *OEDS* for 1937, but must have been widespread by then. Consider the following passage which first appeared in 1904:

I have (said Reginald) an aunt who worries. She's not really an aunt – a sort of amateur one, and they aren't really worries.

(*HHMS*, p. 67)

On the other hand, the relevant meaning is not given in *OED 1*. The *OEDS* says that *auntie* is 'now increasingly used' in this way, but the relevant volume was published in

1972, and by then the custom must have been fading. People of my generation (born just after the Second World War) are familiar with courtesy aunts of this kind; I have often used titles of this kind, but I personally have seldom been addressed by such a courtesy title, nor have my children used one. People who are currently in their early twenties seem to fall into two groups: there are some who find the idea of courtesy aunts and uncles rather quaint, and some who not only have had them, but who are addressed in this way themselves.

Of course, it is not only aunts (and uncles) who cause problems of address. Consider the following citations from university environments. The first, which appeared in 1951, reflects a conservative environment:

Lady Muriel, stiff as she was, would never have called men by their college titles.

(CPSM. p. 61)

In (a Cambridge) college, titles are used between the men, although this may reflect personal relationships:

'May I pour you some sherry, Bursar?' said Jago, not at ease with him.

(CPSM, p. 18)

In a less conservative institution, though in a passage written only a few years later and published in 1954, we find the following comment:

'I don't know, Professor,' he said in sober veracity. No other professor in Great Britain, he thought, set such store by being called Professor.

(KALJ, p. 7)

In the same work, we find professors addressing lecturers by their surnames, while students address them, and are addressed by them, by title and surname:

'Oh, by the way Dixon[.]' Dixon turned to him with real avidity. 'Yes, Professor?'

(KALJ, p. 17)

'Excuse me, Mr Dixon; have you a minute to spare?'
First making his shot-in-the-back face, Dixon stopped and turned. He was leaving College after a lecture, and so had been hurrying. 'Yes, Mr Mitchie?'

Mitchie was a moustached ex-service student ...

(KALJ, p. 27)

In a more recent work, published in 1988, matters have changed considerably. Professors address their lecturers by their given names, and lecturers usually reciprocate in kind, although new lecturers (like Robyn in the passage below) may be in doubt:

'Good morning, Bob. Good morning, Robyn.'
'Oh, hallo, Philip,' says Bob Busby. Robyn merely says 'Hallo'. She is always uncertain how to address her Head of Department. 'Philip' seems too familiar, 'Professor Swallow' too formal, 'Sir' impossibly servile.

(DLNW, pp. 36–7)

It should be noted in passing that the final remark about the servility of 'Sir', while justified in a British context, would probably not be justified in an American one. It comes as a shock to most Americans to learn that many British speakers give up using 'Sir' when they leave school. While it still exists in the service industries and the armed forces in British English, its range has been very much curtailed. The twentieth-century examples of this *Sir* in *OED 2* all come from school contexts. While this is no doubt excessive, it makes a point.

The way in which students are addressed has similarly changed. In a work set in Oxford and published in 1974 we find the following, where the narrator is a former student and Talbert is a lecturer:

I found myself touched that Talbert had addressed me by my Christian name.... I did recall how in my last year ... Talbert himself had taken to addressing me in this more familiar fashion. Nowadays Oxford dons, like young people at a party, know both each other and their pupils by their Christian names alone, so that upon formal occasions they are at a loss as to who is being designated Smith or Brown. Talbert's habits had been formed in an earlier era. For several terms he had invariably addressed me as *Mr* Pattullo.

(JIMS, pp. 14–15)

The 'earlier era' cannot have been much earlier than between the wars, but the custom of addressing undergraduates by title and surname persisted in some British universities at least into the 1970s. I can personally attest that it was the norm at the University of Edinburgh into the 1970s.

Of course, universities are not the only work-places or educational institutions where conventions of address have changed over the years. In schools there seems to have been a move away from addressing boys (in particular) by their surname alone and towards using given names. Consider the following, in which someone is reminiscing about the years 1936–41:

boys were addressed by their surnames, girls by first names. On only one occasion did a master call me Laurie – when he shouted to me to pass a ball in a football match. I was so astounded that I almost didn't pass.

(*The Daily Mail*, 23 September 1989, p. 33, col. 4)

Similar conventions applied into the 1960s, although there were signs of a change in the sixth form at that period. I can remember being put out when one master addressed me by my first name in the mid-sixties, because it seemed to imply a greater degree of intimacy than I felt existed. This general trend towards less formal address systems is not limited to school teachers addressing pupils, but is also true of pupils addressing other pupils who are not intimates. Peter Ustinov recalls modes of address between pupils in about 1928 when he writes of receiving condolences on some team's performance:

'Hard cheese, von Ustinov' from my acquaintances, 'Better luck next time, Oosti' from my friends.

(*PUDM*, p. 72)

Note that he was not addressed as 'Peter' or 'Pete' or by any other version of his given name. While such conventions may persist in a few schools in the 1990s, they are no longer the rule. It used also to be the convention to address workers in the same institution by surname alone, for example in hospitals and commercial offices. This too has faded.

In all these cases, we can view the change as being one of increasing informality: yesterday's informal usage becomes tomorrow's formal usage. This is also the change that we have seen taking place in other areas of language (see, in particular, the discussion in section 1.2). It might also be said to be the direction of change in non-linguistic matters such as dress codes. Whether conventions of address are purely a linguistic matter, or whether they are more like conventions of dress, is, I think, an open question.

5.4 Engineered change

Most of the changes that have been discussed so far in this book are changes which appear to have emerged independent of the wills of the speakers of the language. They have not been changes which are imposed on the language, but cases of the language evolving. Change which is imposed, which is deliberately sought, which is, in effect, engineered, is also found.

One simple example is provided by changes to derogatory words describing ethnic groups. These are words like *dago, Frog, Nigger, Spik, wog* and *Yid*. Like all words, these words have a DENOTATION and a CONNOTATION. The denotation is what they actually refer to, the connotation is the emotional overtones they carry with them. For these derogatory words, the connotation is a vital part of the meaning of the whole. Those referred to by these words have long felt wounded by the use of the terms, and their crusade has been to make the unthinking users of the terms realize just how offensive they are. While the use of the words has not been prevented by these efforts, the crusade has been successful to the extent that these words are now, as the *OEDS* says of *nigger*, 'restricted to contexts of deliberate and contemptuous ethnic abuse'. One sign of the change in attitude to these words in the course of this century is the style labels they are given in the successive editions of the *Concise Oxford Dictionary* (*COD*), listed in Table 5.1.

Among other things to note in Table 5.1 is the change in style labels from 'contemptuous', which indicates the attitude of the speaker, to 'derogatory' which indicates to a far greater degree the effect on the listener. Using *COD* 7 we can find a definition of 'contemptuous' as 'showing the mental attitude of despising', while 'derogatory' is defined as 'involving disparagement or discredit to'. The increasing awareness of the problems these words cause is also clear in other ways, including the introduction of the overtly

Table 5.1 Style marking for various offensive nouns in different editions of *The Concise Oxford Dictionary*

Word	COD 1 (1911)	COD 5 (1964)	COD 6 (1976)	COD 7 (1982)	COD 8 (1990)
dago	no style label	term of contempt	sl., derog.	sl, derog., **R**	sl offens.
frog	contempt. for	derog. for	derog.	derog.	sl offens.
kraut	not listed	not listed	derog.	derog.	sl offens.
nigger	usu. contempt.	usu. derog.	derog.	derog., **R**	offens.
squarehead	not listed	no style label	derog.	derog., **R**	not listed
wog	not listed	sl.	sl., derog.	sl, derog., **R**	sl offens.
wop	not listed	sl.	sl., derog.	sl, derog., **R**	sl offens.
yid	not listed	sl.	sl., derog.	sl, derog., **R**	sl offens.

Note: **R** = 'racially offensive'

prescriptive marking '**R**' in *COD 7*, discarded in favour of the overtly critical term 'offensive' in *COD 8*.

One of the most successful pieces of engineered change this century has been the introduction of the title *Ms* to apply equally to married and unmarried women (just as *Mr* applies to married and unmarried men). The *OEDS* gives a first citation for this form in 1952, though it appears to have caught on in the 1970s. Indeed, feminist-inspired engineered change to remove sexist language has been very successful in the last twenty years in formal institutional language. As a fairly simple example, consider the following regulation from the *Victoria University of Wellington Calendar* as presented in 1980 and in 1990:

Any student who wishes to add a course after the commencement of the academic year must make application on the appropriate form and obtain the approval of the Chairman of Department who approved his course for the year and the lecturer in charge of any course which he wishes to enter.

(VUW Calendar, 1980)

Any candidate who wishes to add a course after the commencement of the academic year must apply on the appropriate form and obtain the approval of the lecturer in charge of the course which the candidate wishes to enter and of the Chairperson of the Department which approved the personal course of study.

(VUW Calendar, 1990)

There are two points worthy of note here: an avoidance of sexist terminology, and an avoidance of *he* to refer to females as well as to males. The change of *Chairman* to *Chairperson* in this regulation is symptomatic of a much wider change away from any label for jobs or functions that implicitly or explicitly refer to the gender of the incumbent: *actress, barmaid, headmaster, lady-doctor, policeman* are all now disfavoured, helped in many countries by legislation which makes it illegal to advertise positions in such a way that people of only one sex will be able to apply (unless there is some very good reason for the job to be gender-specific). Another symptom of this trend is the comment in the introduction to a recent edition of *Roget's Thesaurus*, that

The aim throughout was to mirror the language and attitudes of our present society. This included taking into account the increasing tendency to counter the sexism present in our language by inventing new neutral terms. These, and female equivalents such as 'spokeswoman', have been added to their male counterparts.

(Lloyd, 1982, p. viii)

The law and current attitudes have created a demand for these 'neutral terms', and works such as Lloyd (1982) and a growing number of handbooks on non-sexist language are responding to an increasing demand from English speakers for terms of this kind.

It is not only in vocabulary, however, that a change is needed if sexism is to be eradicated from English. This, too, was illustrated in the university regulations reproduced above with the rather clumsy repetition of *the candidate* in the 1990 version. The problem is that there is no well-established simple way of writing 'he or she', and so on. Fowler (1926, p. 648) states categorically that

the right shortening of the cumbersome *he or she* . . . is *he*.

In the revised edition of the same book, Gowers adds, and cites with approval, the following sentence promulgated by a government department.

There must be opportunity for the individual boy or girl to go as far as his keenness and ability will take him.

(Fowler, 1965, p. 635)

Today such a sentence probably seems absurd. Unfortunately, very often the alternative seems to be the awkward *he or she* (or *she or he*) or, in written but not spoken form, *s/he*. Various attempts have been made to engineer a change here, but most of them have failed dismally. Among suggestions for a sex-neutral pronoun are *co, e, et, hesh, hir* and *thon* (Cheshire, 1985). The only one which shows any sign of being widely used is *they*, as in *as anybody can see for themselves*, a usage which Fowler (1926, p. 392) says 'sets the literary man's teeth on edge'. As Cheshire (1985, p. 25) comments, 'Perhaps a literary woman would be less sensitive!' Although a sentence such as *The end user can design their own instruments* (*SSUM*, 13) still may sound a little odd, especially to older speakers or in formal usage, it seems likely that this is what will become the general usage in a few more years unless attitudes change again.

One result of the consciousness of sexism in formal language is that *she* is being used less to refer to inanimate objects than previously, at least in formal written usage. Colloquial Australian and New Zealand English still retain usages such as *She'll be right!*, and it is still possible in all standard forms of English to refer to ships and cars as *she*, but people are more conscious of such usages than they used to be. One unexpected change, which may be related to this, and certainly has the same overall effect, is a reduction in the use of *she* to refer to countries. In *The Times* corpus (see section 3.1), the use of *she* to refer to countries was the norm until 1930. We find, for instance,

... there are several other points of difference still open between Canada and her great neighbour.

(*The Times*, 7 March 1900, p. 9, col. 6)

Russia has now replaced all her frontier troops.

(*The Times*, 1 March 1905, p. 9, col. 5)

Turkey's proposal to heighten her Customs duties is in the same inconclusive state. If she gets the consent of the Powers she may find it conditioned by restrictions ...

(*The Times*, 1 March 1905, p. 9, col. 5)

Between 1900 and 1930 there were only three cases of *it*

referring back to a country which had been named, all in the 1915 data. From 1935 the usage of *it* increases gradually (though not regularly), until in 1970 *it* becomes the majority form in such cases. *She* is still used, but less so, at least in *The Times*. The figures from *The Times* corpus are presented in Figure 5.1. On 27 November 1989, Mrs Thatcher, then Britain's Prime Minister, was interviewed on the BBC1 'Panorama' programme. She consistently referred to countries using the pronoun *she*. Interestingly enough, it sounded rather old-fashioned, although this usage can still be heard from less obviously conservative speakers.

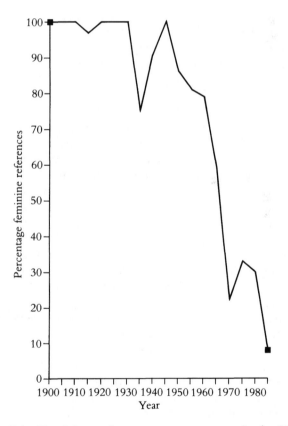

Figure 5.1 Feminine and neuter country names in the *The Times* corpus

The changes that have been discussed in this section are all changes which have taken place or are taking place in formal English. You do not need to be an ardent feminist to realize that sexist terms survive far better in informal spoken language than in formal, institutional language. This is one of the cases where it is the middle classes who are innovating, the change is conscious and provides a prestige form (see section 1.2). It is too early to say how far this change will spread.

5.5   Methodological observations

What the changes discussed in this chapter have in common, and what distinguishes them from the changes discussed in earlier chapters, is that they all appear to have been motivated by changes in society. The linguistic changes seem to be a reflection of social change rather than changes which come from the language system itself. The same could also be said of the idiosyncratic lexical changes mentioned in section 2.1. If, in the 1990s, the word *pantyhose* is current, and the word *doublet* is restricted to historical contexts, this is more a fact about the society of the 1990s than about its language. The language reflects the technology, the attitudes, the philosophy, the structures of the society in which it functions. It is fairly easy to think of areas where changes in technology or in official structures have changed the language. An obvious example is the advent of the micro-processor, which has given us words and phrases (or new meanings for old words and phrases) such as *application*, *disk drive*, *floppy* (noun), *hardware*, *interface*, *modem*, *mouse*, *RAM*, *ROM*, *software*, *throughput*, *user friendly*, *virus*, *WYSIWYG*, and many others. Note that a phrase like *user friendly* has spread far beyond the domain of computing. The *OEDS* has an example of *user friendly* being applied to a family of dolls.

This has implications for what the linguist needs to study. The causes of the changes discussed in this chapter are purely social causes, not linguistic ones. Any search for linguistic explanations of change is thus unlikely to apply to these changes as well. On the other hand, the same ways of recording the changes remain valid, and the same patterns of change are found. That this should be the case is not surprising, given the way in which other kinds of linguistic change are socially mediated. But it is important to note that not all linguistic change can necessarily be explained in terms of the same set of principles.

Reading and References

5.2 Spelling

On spelling reform see Crystal (1987) and McArthur (1992).

5.4 Engineered change

For an excellent introduction to sexism in English, see Cheshire (1985). This is an area which has captured the imagination of the media, as well as linguistic scholars, in the past twenty years, and there is a large amount of material available. As (fairly random) examples from this huge literature, consider Graddol and Swann (1989) (esp. ch. 5), Frank and Anshen (1983) and Frank and Treichler (1989). The last of these contains several bibliographies.

Notes

5.1 Punctuation and formal aspects of writing

Right into the 1940s, *The Times* was marking long quotations with a new set of inverted commas at the beginning of every line of the quotation. This procedure had disappeared by 1950 in favour of a single set of inverted commas at the beginning of the quotation. The old-fashioned format is now found again on electronic bulletin boards and the like, and may thus be making a come-back.

Another area of variation which could indicate change is the emphatic use of quotation marks. Butchers who write in their display windows (in areas where butchers still do this) 'Leg's of "lamb" ', probably believe themselves to be doing no more than using a hand-written version of a typographical 'Legs of Lamb'. *My reaction to such notices* is quite different, and I have heard of others who have the same reaction even though they were brought up (and went to school) on different continents. I treat 'lamb' in such contexts as being enveloped in what I have heard termed scare quotes. Quirk et al. (1985, p. 1635) say that in this usage, quotation marks 'imply that the item is of doubtful validity because merely alleged'. In other words, it looks as though the sign is saying 'This isn't really lamb, but we're calling it that'. The reader is left wondering what the meat really is. This supposedly emphatic use of quotation marks may or may not be innovative: evidence is hard to come by. It is not clear, either, whether it counts as standard or not.

Exercises

1. Find a number of books on letter writing (secretaries' handbooks and the like) published at different times in the course of the century. What differences of layout and punctuation are recommended? Can you date the changes with any accuracy? Is there any apparent reason for the changes?

2. Carry out a survey among your acquaintances to see which of them use or have used the terms 'aunt' and 'uncle' as described in section 5.3, and which of them are addressed in this way. Can you predict on the basis of age, sex, social class, educational level, ethnicity, region of origin or any combination of these whether people will use *aunt* and *uncle* as courtesy titles?

3.* How are boys and girls addressed by teachers in the primary and secondary schools in your area? Does it vary from school to school? Does it correlate with the perceived status of the school? Are boys treated the same way as girls, or differently? How were people of your parents' generation addressed in school? If there has been a change, how closely can you date the change? How do and did school-boys and school-girls address each other, especially when they are (were) not intimates?

4.* See how many sex-neutral and sex-specific job titles you come across in the course of a week. For each, note whether it is in written or spoken language. Does your experience reflect what is done in the Positions Vacant column of your local newspaper?

5.* Collect a number of spelling mistakes from notice-boards, letters, your own essays, the media, and so on. Identify recurrent patterns in the errors. For each pattern, see if you can provide a motivation for the mistake occurring rather than the normatively 'correct' spelling. If there are any particularly common misspellings, why do they not become standard?

CHAPTER 6

Theoretical perspective

6.1 Introduction

In a very influential paper, Weinreich et al. (1968) argue that
a theory of language change involves dealing with four
problems, each of which contributes to our understanding
of what they term the ACTUATION PROBLEM. These four
problems they entitle the problems of constraints, transi-
tion, embedding and evaluation. In what follows, I shall
take each of these and the overall question of actuation one
at a time, explain what is involved, and talk about the way
in which the data sets that have been considered earlier in
the book relate to them.

You will have to realize, though, that the data sets that
we have looked at show a very limited number of types of
process operating. There are many recurrent processes of
change which we have not considered, either because they
do not occur in current standard Englishes, or because they
are difficult to explain and observe, or because it is difficult
to present data which shows clearly what is happening. For
instance, one common change in the histories of many
languages is the replacement of stop consonants between
vowels by fricatives. In Spanish, for instance, what is
written *d* in a word like *todo* 'all', and was historically
pronounced as a [d], is pronounced [ð]. Such changes do
occur in standard varieties of English. If you listen for long
enough, and hard enough, you may hear a *g* in a word like
agapanthus pronounced as a fricative. But this is not (yet?) a
striking feature of spoken English, it tends not to occur in

formal styles, so that it can be difficult to elicit, relevant words are not all that common, and it can sometimes be difficult to decide whether a stop or a fricative has been said. Even if there is change taking place in this area of contemporary English, it would be difficult to provide really useful data about it. Similar examples could be given for a vast number of processes of change. The point is that by examining changes taking place in twentieth-century standard varieties of English, changes which it is relatively straightforward to observe going on, we have excluded a number of possible changes which are of great interest to the student of the processes of language change. There is a lot more to language change than has been discussed in this introductory book.

6.2   The constraints problem

The constraints problem concerns the notion 'possible change'. What is a possible change, and what are the possible conditions for change? For instance, in section 4.4 we saw evidence of the fronting of /uː/ in the course of this century. Would it have been equally possible for /uː/ to have lowered? If so, are there conditions which would have to be met before /uː/ could lower? What conditions, if any, allow /uː/ to front?

Clearly such questions cannot be answered on the basis of the data we have considered here alone. Answers to questions of this kind have to be deduced from the observation of many different actual changes. Such information as we have suggests that it would not, in fact, be equally possible for /uː/ to have lowered, since long peripheral vowels such as /uː/ generally rise (or front or diphthongize) rather than lower (Labov et al., 1972). In other cases, we simply cannot answer the questions. For instance, if preposition stranding is increasing in relative clauses (section 3.4), would it have been equally possible for preposition stranding to decrease, and what conditions lead to one or the other? We do not have sufficient information to say. Studies of preposition stranding in different places in various varieties of English and of comparable phenomena in other languages will be required before we can start making guesses. The study here is, in this sense, part of the data base that is needed to answer the question.

On the other hand, there are some features which are known to constrain the way in which languages change, and one of these, MARKEDNESS, can be illustrated from the data we have already considered. Markedness, however, has been defined in a number of apparently different ways in linguistics, and some explanation is required.

First of all, markedness refers to the presence of a 'mark' in the sense of some linguistic material, frequently an affix. In this sense, *cats* is marked with respect to *cat* because it shows the mark *-s*. Conversely, *cat* is unmarked in relation to *cats* in this sense.

Now, it so happens that *cat* has a wider distribution than *cats*. There are places where *cat* can occur but *cats* cannot: for instance, we can say *cat door* but not *cats door*, even when it is for use by more than one cat. Partly for this reason, *cat* tends to occur more frequently in texts than *cats* does. In the one million words of written American English in the Brown corpus, *cat* occurs fifteen times, *cats* only eleven (Kučera and Francis, 1967); in the one million words of written British English in the LOB corpus, *cat* occurs fifteen times, *cats* only six times (Johansson and Hofland, 1989). These factors of wider distribution and greater text frequency are also associated with unmarkedness.

Where text frequency correlates with lack of a linguistic mark, it is perhaps not surprising that children tend to learn the unmarked term before the marked. Perhaps more surprising is the fact that the same categories (in this case the singular) tend to be unmarked in some or all of these senses across languages and at different times in the evolution of languages.

While these various meanings of marked and unmarked are in principle distinguishable, in practice they are often conflated. Particular phenomena are then said to be NATURAL to the extent that they are regularly unmarked across languages or within one language.

One thing such a notion of naturalness attempts to account for is morphological change, and that is where it is relevant to our concerns here. Recall the change from suffixed to periphrastic in the marking of the comparative discussed in section 3.2. In this case, there are two possible paradigms for comparative formation, the synthetic or suffixed paradigm as in *common, commoner, commonest* and the analytic or periphrastic paradigm, as in *common, more common, most common*. At the beginning of the twentieth century, it was difficult to know how to define the set of adjectives which belonged to each of the two paradigms. Part of the difficulty was caused by the fact that a given adjective did not belong consistently to a single paradigm, but might be compared analytically or synthetically on different occasions. By the end of the period, however, the situation had changed so that adjectives were more likely to belong to one class or the other without vacillation.

We can generalize this change, following Wurzel (1987, p. 80) in terms of INFLECTIONAL CLASS STABILITY. At the beginning of the period, membership of the two paradigms was not predictable, and so neither of the paradigms had a stable membership. In the course of the century, it has become more possible to define the two classes of adjectives in terms of their phonological form. This means there is less uncertainty about which adjective belongs to which paradigm, and the membership of the two classes has become more stable. There is thus a change towards inflectional class stability, a natural state in language. We expect change in inflectional systems, other things being equal, to result in greater inflectional class stability, to lead to an increase in naturalness in this way. This particular case, thus, has an expected result.

Q   *What is the major advantage of inflectional class stability for the person who is studying a language which has such stability as a foreign language?*

A   It means they know which inflectional class any word belongs to; where there are unstable inflectional classes, this cannot be predicted, and so must be learnt along with the word. In fact, most languages have a mixture of stable and unstable inflectional classes.

Naturalness is, however, not only concerned with morphology. In particular, it is worth considering some of the phonological changes reported in Chapter 4. We shall consider the case of the changes of stress (section 4.2). The following comments are extremely superficial, and do not give this question nearly the coverage it might deserve. They may, nevertheless, be suggestive.

The general Germanic stress pattern, which Old English inherited, was for stress to fall on the first syllable of the root of the word (that is, prefixes were in general not stressed). Modern English words like *children, begotten, butter* still reflect this pattern. Since very few Germanic roots in English are of more than two syllables, the Germanic rule does not affect stress in longer (non-compound) words.

With the Norman Conquest and the consequent explosion of Romance vocabulary in English (which persisted until at least the end of the eighteenth century), a Latinate stress rule was imported into English along with the borrowed words. The Latinate stress rule depends on the notion of syllable weight. A heavy syllable is one that contains a long vowel or a diphthong or that is closed by (at least) two consonants. A light syllable contains a short vowel followed by a maximum of one consonant. The Latinate stress rule is then as follows: if the final syllable is heavy, it is stressed; if not, and the penultimate syllable is heavy, it is stressed; if not, the antepenultimate syllable is stressed. Hence the stress falls on one of the final three syllables of the word. Notice that in many cases of disyllabic words in particular the Germanic stress rules and the Latinate stress rules will give the same result.

Q *If the following words are stressed according to the stress rules just given, where will the stress fall in each?* Exempt, refute, Alexander, America, Wellington.

A They would all be stressed as you would expect, as long as the syllable boundary in *Wellington* is drawn between the *ng* and the *t:* ex'empt, re'fute, Alex'ander, A'merica, 'Wellington.

Now consider the words which were used in section 4.2 to show the changing pattern of stress:

(1) abdomen
     acumen
     anchovy
     bitumen
     climacteric
     dirigible
     exigency
     formidable
     fragmentary
     hospitable
     inexplicable
     metallurgy
     molybdenum
     nomenclature
     pejorative
     precedence
     quandary
     secretive
     sonorous
     vagary

In many of these words, there is an involved pattern of
causality since the vowel changes and the stress changes go
hand-in-hand. Both the new and the old stress patterns fit
the Latinate stress rule given above in the case of *abdomen*,
anchovy for instance. This is because there has not only been
a change in stress, but a concomitant change in the vowel
qualities, which have affected syllable weight. However, in
those instances where the words were earlier stressed on the
first syllable of a four-syllable word, there seems to be a
change from a Germanic type of stress-pattern (even though
these are not etymologically Germanic words) to a Latinate
stress pattern. This change could be seen as the generalization
of a stable paradigm for stress to an increasing number of
words; the only oddity in this is referring to stress as
something which occurs in a paradigm (the paradigm
generally being seen as a morphological construct), but the
extension seems perfectly justifiable.

To take this notion further, consider in particular
words which have the suffix -*able*. Morphologically, these
can be divided into two groups, those like *acceptable*,
enjoyable whose base (*accept*, *enjoy*) is transparently recoverable
in the -*able* derivative, and those like *veritable*, *vulnerable*

where the base is not a transparently recoverable English word. There is an apparently intermediate group made up of words like *operable, tolerable* (from *operate, tolerate*) where the suffix *-ate* is deleted (or, more technically, TRUNCATED) from the base before *-able* is added. The general rule for both those words with a transparently recoverable base and for those with truncated *-ate* is that the stress of the *-able* derivative is on the same syllable as the stress of the base word:

(2) ac'cept   ac'ceptable
     'analyse   'analysable
     'manage   'manageable
     'operate   'operable

This is a typical pattern for the most productive types of word-formation in English. In cases where there is no transparently recoverable English base word, however, such a rule cannot apply. The traditional pattern for these words is for the stress to fall two syllables before the *-able* suffix (Fudge, 1984, p. 52):

(3) 'amiable
     in'domitable
     'veritable

There are three interesting cases where the conservative stress assignment is changing.

First, there are some exceptions to the rule that a transparently recoverable base word and its *-able* derivative are stressed on the same syllable. Such words are stressed as if their bases were not transparently recoverable words, with the stress falling two syllables before the suffix.

(4) ad'mire   'admirable
     com'pare   'comparable
     re'voke   (ir)'revocable
     la'ment   'lamentable
     pre'fer   'preferable

Where there is change to such words, it is towards the stable pattern, and these words are being made to fit the general rule.

Secondly, there are some words which have truncated *-ate*, but do not fit the general pattern given above.

(5) 'demonstrate   de'monstrable
     'extricate   ex'tricable

These innovative stress patterns (older stress patterns fitting
the generalizations given above are to be found in *EPD 1*)
show changes putting stress on the antepenultimate syllable,
and thus treating the whole word as unanalysable.

Thirdly, there are cases which used to be covered by
the 'two syllables before the suffix' generalization, and
which no longer are:

(6) ap'plicable
     for'midable
     ho'spitable

Again, these show a change away from the established
pattern towards the more general pattern of antepenultimate
stress. There are a number of analogies which might help
such a change, such as words which only have one syllable
before the affix

(7) 'affable
     'arable
     'capable
     'liable

and words which have an unstressed prefix two syllables
before the affix, and thus look as if they are stressed by an
antepenult rule:

(8) im'mutable
     im'placable
     im'peccable

Q *Why do these only 'look as if' they are stressed by the
antepenult rule?*

A   Because prefixes are not, as a general rule, stressed –
compare the comment on Germanic prefixes earlier. The
stress, therefore, cannot easily be placed further towards the
front of the word than it appears here, whatever rule is
applying. You may be able to think of some counter-
examples, but they are not very common.

There are thus two conflicting patterns of stress change affecting derivatives in -*able*: either they are coming to retain the stress of the base more than before, or they are adopting antepenultimate stress more and more (in many cases, of course, these do not conflict, as is shown by the examples in (4) above). The 'two syllables before the suffix' rule is gradually being lost in favour of more general rules. The net result of this is that the morphological categories and the phonological categories are matching more often than they used to. All words with bases that are non–transparent are beginning to act in the same way, independent of the source of the lack of transparency. In other words, the paradigms are becoming more stable, because they are determined by information from another level of language.

In these cases, then, we can see naturalness as a constraint on the way in which language is changing. Factors such as markedness are extremely important in deciding what is or is not a possible change.

6.3   The transition problem

This problem concerns the way in which language changes. How does a linguistic system move from one state to another? Does the change apply gradually or abruptly, does it apply regularly or irregularly, does it apply across the board or does it apply only to some forms? Part of this problem is whether change operates in terms of lexical diffusion (see section 4.2) or not.

Here we do have some relevant evidence. Consider first the changes to /uː/ mentioned above and discussed in section 4.4. If we make the simplifying assumption that the change to this vowel starts where it is attested at the beginning of the century and finishes where it is last attested, then we seem to have evidence for gradual change, because we have also attested intermediate steps. The evidence that was presented in section 4.4 is also compatible with a sound change operating without any lexical diffusion. This, however, is scarcely surprising. It is not surprising because it was simply assumed in the methodology that any token of /uː/ would be as good as any other in finding out what was happening to /uː/. If the values of /uː/ were very different in two different words, this would not have been noticed, because the two would have been averaged out to provide the value for any speaker.

(This is an important point, and one which has implications far beyond the case in hand. In general, setting up any hypothesis makes background assumptions. Experimental method will only produce valid answers if those background assumptions are correct. But experiments conducted on the basis of these assumptions will not generally be able to prove or disprove them. In setting up experiments, you therefore have to make the best possible assumptions – those that you believe are least likely to cause problems. Sometimes it is impossible to make totally uncontroversial assumptions. Part of the task of assessing the results of experiments is to assess the validity of the background assumptions. This is often a very difficult task. Consequently, experiments can provide answers which are not helpful, despite the best attempts of the experimenters. This applies not only to linguistics, but to all experimental subjects.)

Change which occurs gradually, with intermediate steps and without lexical diffusion is sometimes referred to in the literature as NEO-GRAMMARIAN change, after the neo-grammarians (an English translation of the German term *Junggrammatiker*, a group of German philologists of the 1870s who were the first to put the study of language on a properly scientific footing by looking for fully regular patterns of change in language).

Now consider change to the way comparison of adjectives is expressed (discussed in section 3.2). This does not allow for intermediate steps. There is nothing which is half-way between *commoner* and *more common* (even the non-standard *more commoner* is not really a half-way stage). The change, therefore, must be abrupt not gradual in the individual examples (although there may be gradualness in that there may be vacillation between suffixed and peri-phrastic comparison for any given word). Also, we saw that some words appear to have changed patterns earlier than others: *common* is now generally used with periphrastic comparison, *remote* still seems to be showing more vacillation. Although we did not actually provide direct evidence of lexical diffusion for this change, lexical diffusion seems like a reasonable hypothesis about what is going on in this area.

The distinction between neo-grammarian change and lexical diffusion has given rise to a great deal of discussion where sound change is concerned. Labov (1981) sees here a paradox: sound change appears to operate according to neo-grammarian laws and according to lexical diffusion, yet the two are incompatible because neo-grammarian change implies intermediate stages while lexical diffusion does not. He suggests that the 'paradox' can be resolved by admitting that there are two prototypical kinds of sound change (he allows for intermediate types as well): there is neo-grammarian sound change, which is found in 'low-level output rules' (1981, p. 304), and there is lexical diffusion which affects cases where there are 'changes across subsystems' (1981, p. 303) (e.g. changes from long to short vowels, and so on) or, more generally, when what Labov calls one 'abstract word class' is redistributed into others (1981, p. 304). In a more recent paper, Harris (1989, p. 55) suggests that it may be possible to see these two types of sound change as a single process, but with the neo-grammarian type being the more superficial type of change and leading to the less superficial diffusionist type with the passing of time.

In Chapter 4, three sound changes were considered: vowel changes, stress changes and yod-dropping. Vowel change of the type discussed in section 4.4 is a type of change which Labov finds usually to be of the neo-grammarian kind. As stated above, the findings here were compatible with that, but are not conclusive evidence. The stress change considered in section 4.2 is phonetically abrupt, not phonetically gradual: there is no intermediate stage between *'controversy* and *con'troversy* (unless, perhaps it is full vowels in both syllables). We would thus expect to find this a case of lexical diffusion, and indeed it was used to illustrate this type of propagation of a change. The case of yod-dropping discussed in section 4.3 is, on the face of it, another phonetically abrupt change. In this case, though, phonetically intermediate forms are perfectly possible. For example, [tʲuːn] (with a palatalized [t] but no [j]) would be an intermediate stage between /tjuːn/ and /tuːn/, and such intermediate forms are found. It does seem, though, that these are perceived as belonging either to /tjuːn/ or to /tuːn/, and only the categorial distinctions are regularly reported in the handbooks.

Thus, if the data presented in Chapter 4 cannot be said to support Labov's hypothesis about different kinds of sound change, it certainly does not conflict with it. Where it might provide some solid evidence, though, is in the question raised by Harris of whether the 'deep' category-changing type of change arises from neo-grammarian sound change with time.

The most interesting change for examining this hypo-thesis is the change to stress discussed in section 4.2. As was explained in section 6.2, what is involved is the adoption of Latinate stress patterns in English vocabulary. There is thus a category change from Germanic to Latinate for the words in question. Since this is a change from one abstract word class to another, we would expect to be dealing here with a change by lexical diffusion, for which we have seen there is considerable evidence. The point to note in terms of Harris's theory, though, is that we have no evidence at all of a neo-grammarian type sound change in this instance. This might not be crucial, for it might be the case that the neo-grammarian phase of this sound change was present during the Middle English or Early Modern English periods, at times when the influence of Romance was more strongly felt in English than it is today. However, as was stated above, it is not easy to see how stress shift could occur imperceptibly. The most obvious mechanism would be for the language to shift so that contrastive stress in varied positions in the word vanished and was then re-introduced, but not only is there no evidence for such a shift, if there had been such a shift a larger proportion of the vocabulary might have been expected to change, and to change regularly. We thus have a situation where the evidence appears to suggest that the 'deep' change of stress patterns did not begin as a superficial change at all. While this does not show that such a path is never followed, it does indicate that such a path need not be followed, and thus that Harris's suggestion on the propagation of sound change cannot be the only way in which change can spread.

6.4 The embedding problem

The embedding problem concerns the linguistic system and the social setting in which a change occurs. In terms of embedding within the linguistic system we can ask: What other changes are associated with the given changes in a manner that cannot be attributed to chance? (Weinreich et al., 1968: p. 101). In terms of embedding in social structure we can ask how change is correlated with social factors and whether changes take place in individuals or communities (Labov et al., 1972: p. 9).

6.4.1 Embedding in linguistic structure 1: vowel shifts

One place where we have touched on changes which are correlated with each other was in section 4.4 in the discussion of changes to /æ/. In the discussion of these changes, we pointed out that /æ/ appears to have raised in the earlier part of the century and then to have lowered and retracted in the latter part. Wells (1982, p. 291) points out that similar changes have also affected /e/ and /ı/ in RP: 'Relatively close and peripheral qualities are associated particularly ... with old-fashioned RP; relatively open and central qualities are common with younger speakers'. Wells also comments that there is presumably a link between the qualities of these short front vowels.

Although such a link is not absolute, in that there are varieties of English (like Birmingham) which have relatively close /ı/ without a correspondingly raised /e/ and other varieties (such as New York City) which have a relatively raised /æ/ without a correspondingly close /e/, these vowels do seem to behave in similar manners in a wide range of varieties of English. There is a widespread assumption that this is a causal link, and that these vowels act as a subsystem of vowels which shift as a unit, thus keeping the same phonetic distance between the vowels, but not the same absolute qualities for the vowels. If this did not happen, they would run the risk of encroaching on each other's space, and possibly of merging. In the later part of the century there is some limited evidence that this may be happening with /ʌ/ and /æ/ in RP, since /æ/ has moved down and back and /ʌ/ has moved forward to such an extent that they can now be pronounced in the same part of the vowel area. If this change continues, *cut* and *cat* will be pronounced identically in another half-century or so.

Changes to the other vowels we considered earlier may also be part of chain shifts in the same way, but it is less clear what the system is or that the outcome is going to be so similar in so many varieties of English. The fronting of /uː/ may be related to a raising of /ɔː/ in varieties like New Zealand English, and it is tempting to link the fronting of /ʌ/ with the raising of /æ/ in varieties like Australian, South African and Cockney English, although the evidence is not really strong enough to allow this (Bauer, 1992).

Certainly, it is the case that chain shifts in which whole subsystems of vowels move while remaining distinct are common in language change. They are not, however, inevitable. Merger of two vowels is also a possibility. This brings us back to the constraints problem: under what circumstances will each of these happen? One standard answer to this depends on FUNCTIONAL LOAD. Two vowels will not merge, the theory goes, if they serve to keep a lot of words distinct; they are more likely to merge if they do not have a lot of work to do in keeping messages distinct. So the merger of /ʊə/ and /ɔː/, such that *sure* and *shore* sound the same, is made more likely because these two sounds do not distinguish many words (especially not in context). A merger of /æ/ and /e/, on the other hand, would be far more confusing, and is consequently far less likely to happen. One consequence of this theory, though, is that it would seem to predict that the merger of /æ/ and /ʌ/ in RP will not continue, since those two vowels seem to have a relatively high functional load.

Q   Do you think /æ/ and /ʌ/ will merge in RP or not, given that there are two contradictory forces at work?

A   It is impossible to tell; it depends on how strong each of the forces is. But if you wait twenty years, you may have a better idea.

6.4.2 Embedding in linguistic structure 2: drift

The other place where we seem to have a pattern of changes taking place together concerns the change from suffixed to periphrastic marking of comparison. In more general terms, there has been a change in the history of English from the synthetic use of inflectional endings to the analytic use of periphrases and extra words. The question we need to answer here is whether there is a definite pattern operating or not.

In section 3.2, discussing the change from synthetic comparison to analytic comparison with certain adjectives, I stated that

> The change in the course of this century appears to have been only incidentally an increase in the use of periphrastic comparison. Rather, the change has been a regularization of a confused situation, so that it is becoming more predictable which form of comparison must be used.

But this is to beg the whole question of 'drift' (Sapir, 1921) or linguistic conspiracies (Kisseberth, 1970; Lass, 1974). Can language change be teleological? Why do languages appear to change in a particular direction? Can language change have a particular aim in view, as it were, from the outset?

> The drift of a language is constituted by the unconscious selection on the part of its speakers of those individual variations that are cumulative in some special direction.
>
> (Sapir, 1921, p. 155)

But how can that be? If we follow this through, and view the change as directed in some way, are we not, as Sapir asks, imputing 'a certain mystical quality' to language change (Sapir, 1921, p. 154)?

Q *Why would this be so mystical?*

A Because it would be imputing volition to language, which is not generally considered something which can 'want' to go in any particular direction.

Let us consider the case in hand, the change from synthesis in Old English to analysis in Modern English. Old English was a fusional language. The verb inflected for mood, tense, person and number, the noun inflected for case, and had different paradigms for three genders, the adjective inflected for gender and case and had both weak and strong paradigms, there were dual pronouns, and articles inflected, too. The Modern English verb inflects for tense, and in the non-past for number in the third person singular only (except with the verb to BE). If we assume with most modern linguists that the genitive is not an inflection in Modern English, but a clitic, the noun does not inflect for case. Adjectives inflect only for comparison (the change under consideration). Articles do not inflect. Pronouns show less variation for case and gender than they did in Old English. However, Modern English shows much more fixed word-order than Old English had, makes far greater use of periphrastic verbal constructions (*What are you doing? Her work having been completed, she left*, etc.), makes greater use of prepositions, and uses (the change under discussion) analytic comparison with some adjectives. Can this pattern of changes be explained without recourse to mysticism?

Vennemann (1975) argues that it can. The argument is a complex one, but can be summarized as follows. Case marking on English nouns disappears gradually because of well-known processes of phonetic erosion. Germanic languages are particularly prone to this because they stress the initial syllables in words, leaving the ends of words unstressed. Once case marking has disappeared, the difference between subject and object cannot be discerned from the shape of the word. This is crucial for human interaction. We need to know whether Pat hit Sam or Sam hit Pat (and similarly for a whole range of transitive verbs). It appears that it is a universal in language to put the topic early in the sentence. In most sentences, the topic is the subject. There is thus only a small step to interpreting the first Noun Phrase in the sentence as the subject rather than as the topic. That this has happened in English is shown by the reinterpretation of constructions such as *Me thinks that* ..., where *me* is the object, to *I think that* ..., where *I* is the subject.

At this point, the typical transitive clause has the form

NP NP V, where the first NP is the subject, but neither NP is case-marked. That means that a sentence of the form *Laurie Vivian knows* means 'Laurie knows Vivian' at this stage in the development of the language. But consider a sentence like *The person Chris saw Lee kissed*. At a time when NP NP V order is the norm, the reader or listener meeting this sentence is likely to interpret the first four words as meaning that the person saw Chris, and then be unable to interpret the rest. But the intended reading is one in which *Chris saw* is a relative clause, and the sentence should be interpreted, in such a system, as 'the person who Chris saw kissed Lee'. Such difficulties in processing, Vennemann suggests, lead to the abandonment of NP NP V in favour of NP V NP, where the position relative to the verb defines the difference between subject and object.

Such a change, however, has the effect of upsetting the typological applecart. It is well-known that languages with the order Subject Object Verb differ in a number of crucial respects from languages with the normal order Subject Verb Object. Vennemann relates these differences to the relative order of head and modifier in all constructions. Once a change to Subject Verb Object has taken place, there is pressure within the system for the language to adopt the appropriate relative order of head and modifier in all constructions. Of course, such an enormous change does not happen overnight. In fact, Vennemann suggests, it is still going on, and the change from synthetic to analytic comparison is just one more step in this adjustment. Vennemann (1975, p. 301) relates this specifically to the construction *X is Adj-er than Y* (for example, *Kim is taller than Evelyn*). Using *H* to stand for 'head' and *M* to stand for 'modifier' he diagrams the change from Old English to present-day English in the following terms:

```
(9)  NPCase  +  Adj  +  ER →  MORE  +  Adj  +  THAN  +  standard
      |   |       |      |       |        |       |          |
      M   H       M      H       H        M       H          M
      |  /        \     /        \       /        \         /
         M            H             H             M
```

If we accept this view of the matter, then the change from synthetic to analytic, while it is still not a general change, cannot be dismissed as 'incidental' at all. Rather this drift can be seen as the underlying cause of the current situation, and it may be predicted (with all the provisos that entails, see section 1.3) that the present situation will not persist, but that the analytic comparative will generally take over from the synthetic in all areas.

The nice point about Vennemann's discussion of drift is that it provides us with an explanation of the gradual change from synthetic to analytic without appealing to the mystical, without attributing to speakers a knowledge of the direction in which their language is heading, and without attributing to language, as an entity, any sense of volition. Until we have a constraining theory of the type that Vennemann attempts to provide, the changes can be bewildering. Within an appropriate theory, they can make perfectly good sense. It is why we need to continue the search for appropriate theories concerning language change.

6.4.3 Embedding in social structure

In this book we have adopted without argument the view of social structure presented by Labov. According to this view, changes may be introduced at any social level, but are more likely to spread from less formal styles to more formal styles, and from lower classes to upper classes. Exceptions are cases like the use of non-sexist language discussed in section 5.4 where the innovative form has some kind of overt high prestige. According to this view, the role of the social group is paramount, the role of the individual relatively unimportant. Such a view is controversial. We shall return to an alternative view in section 6.6. Note, however, that because we have simply assumed this view, we have not found evidence about it one way or the other. It was one of the background assumptions that we made.

6.5 The evaluation problem

The evaluation problem concerns the effects of linguistic change. What is the effect of language change on the linguistic system or upon the efficiency of the communication system? This is an area where lay people tend to assume that answers are more easily defined than linguists do. At the beginning of the century, though, even professional linguists saw this as being a fairly straightforward question to answer – even if they did not always agree.

After pointing out that English has changed beyond all recognition since the time of Proto-Indo-European, the Danish grammarian Otto Jespersen (1909, p. 3) asks:

But if the old order has thus changed, yielding place to the new, the question naturally arises: Which of these two is the better order? Is the sum of these infinitesimal modifications which have led our language so far away from the original state to be termed evolution or dissolution, growth or decay?

The question is one with which most modern readers would probably sympathize; many lay people writing about language appear to assume automatically that the answer is clear – change is decay, the language is going to the dogs. This is the view against which Jespersen argues in the book just cited. He contends that English is changing for the better.

Most modern linguists, however, would argue that the question is not answerable. They might follow Hamlet, and say that 'There's nothing either good or bad but thinking makes it so'. That is, goodness or badness of any change depends entirely on the viewpoint of the observer. Change in itself is neutral, neither inherently good nor bad. Whether you stress *abdomen* on the first or second syllable, whether you say *commoner* or *more common*, whether you create animate or inanimate nouns in *-ee* makes absolutely no difference to the efficiency of communication using the language system. You will still be able to say everything you want to say, although you may now say it in a slightly different way. Occasionally you may find language users who exploit language change for their own ends: they blind their audience with science, deliberately obfuscate or mislead, for reasons of propaganda or to further their own commercial interests. But even though language permits these misuses, it does not demand them, and modern language demands them no more than old-fashioned language did. The fact that you can now have legal documents written in plain English, which say the same things as the rather older documents written in obscure legalese makes the point that new English does not automatically have to be more misleading than older English.

This is the sense in which linguists sometimes say that all fully-fledged languages are equal; every language at every stage of its development serves the communicative needs of its speakers. A language before a particular change and after that change will still be able to meet the communicative needs of the speakers. In this sense a change is neither an improvement nor a decline; it is simply a change.

Q *Is it correct to say that standard English and non-standard English are equal because they both serve the needs of the people who use them, or standard English and non-standard English are unequal, because standard English is used by the powerful?*

A Both, but there is some equivocation on the use of the word *equal*, which is what gives rise to the arguments between linguists and lay people. For linguists, the two are equal in serving the function of communication. For lay people, the two are unequal because the functions Standard English serves are thought of as superior to the functions non-Standard English serves.

The only time when efficiency might be impaired is during the course of the change. While the change is on-going, there will be an apparent choice of ways of 'saying the same thing' and just occasionally (as with changes still not complete in standard Englishes to the meanings of *disinterested* and *uninterested*) there may be genuine misunderstandings been conservative and innovative speakers. Consider one case where this seems to be a real problem. New Zealand English has inherited, from its British dialect origins, two meanings for the phrase 'next Thursday'. Spoken on a Tuesday, it can either mean 'the next Thursday we come to', so two days later (this is the English meaning), or it can mean 'Thursday of next week', so nine days later (this is the Scottish meaning). There is variation among New Zealand speakers in the way they use this expression, which probably indicates change in progress, though it is not clear at this stage which direction the change is taking. Clearly, either meaning is a possible one, and if only one meaning existed (whichever it was) communication would be efficient. Equally clearly, it is possible to avoid the issue by saying 'in two days' time' or 'in nine days' time', or by using the phrases 'this Thursday' and 'Thursday of next week'. This is presumably how the variation has managed to last for a hundred and fifty years in New Zealand. That is, despite the variation and the apparent inefficiency it can cause, it seems that, most of the time, it does not cause problems of communication. What variation of this kind does show is that New Zealand English is a living language. In other cases, though not in this particular case, variation is also taken to have a social function, helping to pin-point the speaker socially or regionally, for example. This function of language should not be overlooked. It seems that human language users see this function as so important, that a totally homogeneous communication system is not seen as desirable. In the words of Weinreich et al. (1968, p. 101) 'It is *absence* of structural heterogeneity that would be dysfunctional.' The result of this is change.

Thus it is no longer clear how the linguist is to evaluate language change. All we know is that the matter is not as simple a one as people used to believe.

6.6 The actuation problem

The actuation problem is the crucial question facing students of language change, and to some extent presupposes answers to the other problems that have been raised. Weinreich et al. (1968, p. 102) phrase the question as follows:

Why do changes in a structural feature take place in a particular language at a given time, but not in other languages with the same feature, or in the same language at other times?

Why, that is, should changes to stress patterns or the marking of comparison be taking place in the twentieth century and not the eighteenth? If standard Spanish [g] between vowels has become a fricative, why has the same thing not happened to the same extent in standard Englishes?

We cannot answer this question. But that does not mean that we do not have some ideas about the kind of thing that is going on. Milroy (1992) suggests a partial answer which is likely to be added to and modified in the next few years. He suggests that speech communities have core members who share all the values of the group and interact only sporadically with people from outside the community. They also have peripheral members, who interact much more frequently with people from other speech communities. Because these peripheral members are more exposed to external varieties of English, they are the ones who adopt extraneous innovations, and introduce them to the core members. The core of any speech community, though, is conservative – that is why regional and social dialects persist despite the fact that peripheral members have been using standard forms for centuries. The core members adopt only a very small percentage of the changes that are available to them, probably the ones which are introduced by a large number of peripheral members at about the same time. Only when the core members of a community begin to adopt a feature do we have language change.

Given this kind of picture, we can see why Spanish should have changed intervocalic stops to fricatives but not English: even if the change is available, it is not adopted by the core members of the community in one case, but is in the other. Whether adoption or non-adoption is purely a random matter or whether there are factors which make it easier for innovations to be adopted is an important, and at this stage an open, question. It seems likely that there are at least social factors which make the adoption of some potential innovations more likely than the adoption of others. We can also see why a change should arise in the twentieth rather than the eighteenth century: even if the potential for change is there, there is no change until the core members of a speech community start to adopt it.

To a certain extent, this model of innovation is much more centred on the individual than the community-based model of Labov. But it still leaves open the question of why the community as a whole adopts a change at one point rather than at another. Also, Milroy's model is constructed on the basis of what happens in non-standard speech communities. Some standard speech communities have a similar in-group of core members – those who have attended the major public schools and the Oxbridge universities in Britain, for example, and who form the proverbial 'old-boy network'. But in other speech communities, such as Australia or Canada, it is far less clear that there is a core of speakers of the standard who do not have frequent links with speakers from less standard speech communities. The theory will have to develop to take account of factors such as these.

6.7 Limitations and prospect

The factors just discussed have had clear implications in areas of sound change and grammatical change (especially morphological change). Their implications in terms of lexical change are far less obvious. Where engineered changes, including spelling changes, are concerned some of the factors do not apply in the same way at all. So while the method of adopting a change in a community may be the same, factors such as markedness do not necessarily have any application in such instances. These limitations, of course, do not mean that the points that have been discussed above have no value; they merely indicate that it is important to know how far the influence of some of these factors extends.

Little has been said in this chapter about many of the processes of change which form the core area of study in many more advanced historical linguistics texts: analogical levelling, assimilation, dissimilation, epenthesis, haplology, lenition, metathesis, pidginization and so on, which we could have discussed under the heading of the constraints problem, but which have not been relevant for the material we have considered in this book. An understanding of such processes is crucial for a full understanding of language change, but not for an understanding of what is changing in standard English at the moment.

It will be clear to you that many gaps have been left, both theoretical gaps and descriptive gaps. Theoretically we have raised questions about, for instance, how we evaluate language change, and left them unanswered. Descriptively, we have raised questions about, for instance, whether relative clauses are being used more to refer to human nouns, and left them unanswered. Lack of answers to such questions should not dismay you. Rather, these lacks indicate opportunities. We know a lot about the way English is changing in particular and about the way in which language changes in general. But there is a lot we do not know. Some of these gaps will be filled within the next fifty years or so. If these are questions which strike you as interesting and worthwhile, you could help in answering them. There are opportunities for research here. You might like to carry out some of it.

Reading and References

6.2   The constraints problem

The discussion of stress shift and -able is based firmly on the description given by Fudge (1984). Most of the material on markedness is dealt with in the literature under the heading of 'natural morphology'. For a textbook introduction to natural morphology, see Bauer (1988a, pp. 187–99). A wider-ranging, though still introductory, discussion can be found in Dressler et al. (1987).

The history of English stress and the formulation of the general English stress rules are based on Lass (1987a, p. 108–18).

6.3   The transition problem

Although any textbook on historical linguistics will give an introduction to the neo-grammarians (Bynon, 1977, is a good one), for the discussion of the paradox, you need to read Labov (1981), which is not elementary. For an introduction to lexical diffusion, see the works cited with reference to section 4.2.

On the fact that there are intermediate stages between /tuːn/ and /tjuːn/, see Kelly and Local (1989, pp. 139–40). Kelly and Local imply that standard phonology is not capable of dealing with such facts.

6.4   The embedding problem

Vowel shifts are discussed in greatest detail by Labov et al. (1972), though this work is neither easily available nor easily understood. The principles behind vowel shifts are discussed in most textbooks, usually with reference to the Great Vowel Shift which affected English in about the fifteenth century. For discussion of the modern changes in vowel shift terms, see Bauer (1979).

The best place to start any reading on drift is with the famous chapter from Sapir (1921). Lakoff (1972) formulates the problems for the descriptive linguist well, and brings in a lot of extra data, but the paper is quite strongly criticized by Vennemann (1975). Lass (1974) also considers the methodological problems, especially in his epilogue, and returns to them again in Lass (1987b). The main text on the typological issues is Greenberg (1966), but Comrie (1981) provides a better introduction.

Notes

6.2   The constraints problem

The discussion of stress shift is simplified in as much as it only considers -able derivatives with verbal bases. There is also a relatively large number of denominal -able derivatives, which largely seem to go unrecognized in the literature. *Knowledgeable* is familiar, but examples with truncation, such as *charitable, miserable, memorable, remediable, reputable* are less frequently recognized, as are de-adjectival examples such as *commensurable*. In most cases, the same rules as apply to the de-verbal derivatives seem to apply, but '*reputable* from *re'pute* is a problem.

The discussion in this chapter makes no allowance for a change of the type '*justifiable→justi'fiable* listed by Ramsaran (1990, p. 188). Although the change is a change to antepenultimate stress, as discussed in section 4.2, it appears to be a step away from the predictable paradigms suggested in this chapter. While there could be various reasons for this, I have no suggestions at the moment about which of them might be correct.

6.4 The embedding question

The explanation of the drift from synthetic to analytic given in section 6.4.2 is from Vennemann (1975), but it ignores a considerable amount of work in this area. For example, it should be noted that there could be argument about the way in which Vennemann assigns the labels 'head' and 'modifier' (see discussion in Zwicky, 1985; Hudson, 1987; Bauer, 1990), and that not everyone would agree about the weight of the typological forces. Comrie (1981, pp. 89–96) provides an easily comprehensible discussion of these issues. It should also be asked why, if Vennemann is correct that it was the change to Subject Verb Object from Subject Object Verb which started the drift from synthetic to analytic, there were prepositions in Germanic before this change, since prepositions correlate with Subject Verb Object order, not with Subject Object Verb order.

Suggested answers to exercises

1 Introduction

1. There are so many changes that have occurred since the Old English extract that it is hard to focus on them.

   In spelling, Old English still has the letters thorn (þ) and *asc* (æ) and long vowels (marked with a macron). Where words are still recognizable there are differences of spelling such as *ond* for *and*, *drince* for *drink*, *scancan* for *shanks*, *þurh* for *through* and so on. These reflect differences of pronunciation.

   There are grammatical differences such as the word-order in the first few words. Literally 'if you wolf's-bane eat', and in the endings such as *-an* and *-e* on various words.

   There are changes of vocabulary in that several words such as *þung* have now vanished, and we would be unlikely to talk about 'shanks' these days.

   The Middle English passage retains the thorn, and uses the letter 'y' in many places where we would today use 'i'. It also uses 'v' for 'u' at the beginning of a word. The use of double letters is rather different from current practice.

   The use of *is appeared* rather than *has appeared* is a grammatical feature which differentiates the two kinds of English.

   There are various words such as *garryng* and *grisbittyng* which have vanished.

   Some features of the Shakespearean passage were commented on in the text. Note that the spellings here do not reflect grossly different pronunciations from those we are used to.

   Where vocabulary is concerned, *meat* now means 'flesh of animals' and not just 'food', and we use *laces* not *ribbons* for shoes.

   The passage from Pope is minimally different from

modern English, but note the use of capital letters, the construction *If we would copy* instead of *If we want to copy* and the use of *at this day* instead of *today*.

2 Lexical change

1. You should be able to find some evidence of change for any of these formatives. Some, like *-gate*, arise and go out of fashion quickly. Others, like *-(o)holic*, start this century, but seem well established. Some like *-scape*, never form many words. The attributive nouns are the hardest to deal with, partly because it is hardest to get good data in this area.
2. The task is surprisingly hard. Many words seem to fit into more than one category, or to fit partly into more than one category. You may feel the need to create new categories.
3. The most obvious reason for differences is the period the book covers. Algeo (1991) covers some 50 years, Green (1991) only 30, and Ayto (1990) only a small time period. Also, some works may be more liberal in including compounds, phrases and new uses of old forms than others.

3 Grammatical change

1. Studies by my own students suggest that there is change towards the use of the *-'s* marker.

   This does not really affect the discussion of a general trend from analytic to synthetic, though. Just because there is a general trend in a particular direction, it does not mean that everything must fit that trend. The question of *why* this should stand out against the trend is the kind of question that is not easily answered.
4. We would predict that pronominal concord used more plurals than verbal concord; pronouns seems to be more likely to follow notional concord rather than grammatical (see Corbett, 1983).
6. It is frequently difficult to find clear and specific comments on a particular point in letters to the editor, even though such comments are made fairly regularly. If your teacher has a file of such material, you may be better to start there.

   Finding out whether something is an Americanism can also be difficult. Where vocabulary is concerned the *OED* is the best starting point. For points of grammar, try Quirk et al. (1985). In either case, you may need to check whether the alleged Americanism has fore-runners in Scottish or Irish English. *The Scottish National Dictionary* is of help here.

Trudgill and Hannah (1982) may be of some help in dealing with grammar.

It may also be of interest that many genuine Americanisms are accepted without any difficulty by even the most prescriptive of complainants.

I suspect that many of the self-appointed watchdogs of English usage do not actually know whether a particular usage comes from America or not, but simply use 'American' as a term of abuse. This is impossible to prove, unfortunately.

7. The expected answer is 'Yes', but only your work will say whether this is correct or not. If your answer is not 'Yes', you may like to see if there are any obvious reasons for the normal predictions to fail.

8. How much change you find may depend on how much data you consider. For small amounts of data, there should be little sign of change. Clear signs of change will demand large amounts of data. If you spread the data-collection among several researchers, make sure they are all looking for the same kinds of material.

4 Sound change

8. You will need to listen carefully to do this exercise. Speakers are unlikely to imitate the pronouncing dictionaries, if only because they are likely to vary more.

11. Relevant words occur infrequently, and you may not find enough data unless you actively elicit words from an elderly speaker. Remember the possibility of lexical diffusion, so that you cannot assume from the pronunciation of *dew* that you know how *due* will be pronounced.

15. You would need to test young speakers of standard varieties and some older speakers, and you would need to test them on some words where you expected variation. You would then expect more of the younger speakers to use antepenultimate stress or forms without yod. You would expect some cases where the younger speakers used antepenultimate stress or forms without yod over, say, 60 per cent of the time, still to be listed in dictionaries with a different stress pattern or with /j/.

References

General works, lexica and sources of data

General works

Abercrombie, David (1964) *English Phonetic Texts*. London: Faber and Faber.

Adamson, Doug (1989) 'Cognitive and social constraints on relative clause production.' Paper presented at NWAVE-XVIII, Durham, NC, October 1989.

Aldrich, Ruth I. (1964) '*-Mobile*', *American Speech*, **39**, 77–9.

Aldrich, Ruth I. (1966) 'The development of '-scape'', *American Speech*, **41**, 155–7.

Algeo, John (1980) 'Where do the new words come from?' *American Speech*, **55**, 264–77.

Algeo, John (1991) *Fifty Years Among the New Words*. Cambridge: Cambridge University Press.

Algeo, John and Doyle, Charles Clay (1981a) 'More *-gates*', *American Speech*, **56**, 151–2.

Algeo, John and Doyle, Charles Clay (1981b) 'More *-holics*', *American Speech*, **56**, 152–3.

Allan, W. Scott (1987) 'Lightfoot noch einmal', *Diachronica*, **4**, 123–57.

Ayto, John (1990) *The Longman Register of New Words. Volume 2*. London: Longman.

Bache, Carl and Jakobsen, Leif Kvistgaard (1980) 'On the distinction between restrictive and non-restrictive relative clauses in modern English', *Lingua*, **52**, 243–67.

Bailey, Charles-James N. (1977) Variation and linguistic analysis, *Papiere zur Linguistik*, **12**, 5–56.

Barber, Charles (1964) *Linguistic Change in Present-Day English*. Edinburgh and London: Oliver and Boyd.

Barnhart, David K. (1980) '*Gate* stays open', *American Speech*, **55**, 77–8.

Bauer, Laurie (1979) 'The second Great Vowel Shift?' *Journal of the International Phonetic Association*, **9**, 57–66.

Bauer, Laurie (1982) 'That vowel shift again', *Journal of the International Phonetic Association*, **12**, 48–9.

Bauer, Laurie (1983) *English Word-formation*. Cambridge: Cambridge University Press.

Bauer, Laurie (1985) 'Tracing phonetic change in the received pronunciation of British English', *Journal of Phonetics*, **13**, 61–81.

Bauer, Laurie (1987) '-Ee, by gum!', *American Speech*, **62**, 315–9.

Bauer, Laurie (1988a) *Introducing Linguistic Morphology*. Edinburgh: Edinburgh University Press.

Bauer, Laurie (1988b) 'What is lenition?' *Journal of Linguistics*, **24**, 381–92.

Bauer, Laurie (1990) 'Be-heading the word', *Journal of Linguistics*, **26**, 1–31.

Bauer, Laurie (1992) 'The second Great Vowel Shift revisited', *English World-Wide*, **13**, 253–68.

Bauer, Laurie (1993a) 'Progress with a corpus of New Zealand English and some early results.' In Clive Souter and Eric Atwell (eds), *Corpus-Based Computational Linguistics*. Amsterdam and Atlanta: Rodopi, 1–10.

Bauer, Laurie (1993b) *Manual of Information to Accompany the Wellington Corpus of Written New Zealand English*. Wellington: Department of Linguistics, Victoria University.

Bayard, Donn (1989) ' "Me say that? No way!": the social correlates of American lexical diffusion in New Zealand English', *Te Reo*, **32**, 17–60.

Bell, Allan (1984) 'Language style as audience design', *Language in Society*, **13**, 145–204.

Bell, Allan (1988) 'The British base and the American connection in New Zealand media English', *American Speech*, **63**, 326–44.

Biesenbach-Lucas, Sigrun (1987) 'The use of relative markers in modern American English.' In Keith M. Denning, Sharon Inkelas, Faye C. McNair-Knox and John R. Rickford (eds), *Variation in Language: NWAV-XV at Stanford*, Stanford: Department of Linguistics, Stanford University, pp. 13–21.

Bloomfield, Leonard (1933) *Language*. London: George Allen and Unwin.

Bloomfield, Morton W. and Newmark, Leonard (1963) *A Linguistic Introduction to the History of English*. New York: Alfred A. Knopf.

Brown, Gillian (1977) *Listening to Spoken English*. London: Longman.

Burchfield, Robert (1981) *The Spoken Word: a BBC guide*. London: BBC.

Bynon, Theodora (1977) *Historical Linguistics*. Cambridge: Cambridge University Press.

Chambers, J.K. and Trudgill, Peter (1980) *Dialectology*. Cambridge: Cambridge University Press.

Chen, Matthew (1972) 'The time dimension: contribution toward a theory of sound change', *Foundations of Language*, **8**, 457–98. (Reprinted in Wang (ed.), (1977) pp. 197–251.)

Cheshire, Jenny (1978) 'Present tense verbs in Reading English.' In Trudgill (ed.), (1978) pp. 52–68.

Cheshire, Jenny (1985) 'A question of masculine bias', *English Today*, **1**, 22–6.

Chomsky, Noam and Halle, Morris (1968) *The Sound Pattern of English*. New York: Harper and Row.

Coates, Jennifer and Cameron, Deborah (eds) (1988) *Women in their Speech Communities*. London: Longman.

Comrie, Bernard (1981) *Language Universals and Linguistic Typology*. Oxford: Blackwell.

Corbett, Greville G. (1983) *Hierarchies, Targets and Controllers: agreement patterns in Slavic*. London: Croom Helm.

Coupland, Nikolas (1988) *Dialect in Use*. Cardiff: University of Wales Press.

Crystal, David (1987) *The Cambridge Encyclopedia of Language*. Cambridge: Cambridge University Press.

Dierickx, Jean (1970) 'Why are plural attributives becoming more common?' In Jean Dierickx and Yves Lebrun (eds), *Linguistique Contemporaine*, Bruxelles, 39–46.

Dobson, E.J. (1957) *English Pronunciation 1500–1700*. Oxford: Clarendon Press. Two volumes.

Dressler, Wolfgang U. (1987) 'Word formation as part of natural morphology.' In Dressler et al., pp. 99–126.

Dressler, Wolfgang U., Mayerthaler, Willi, Panagl, Oswald and Wurzel, Wolfgang U. (1987) *Leitmotifs in Natural Morphology*. Amsterdam and Philadelphia, PA: Benjamins.

Fowler, H.W. (1926) *A Dictionary of Modern English Usage*. Oxford: Clarendon Press. (Reprinted 1959.)

Fowler, H.W. (1965) *A Dictionary of Modern English Usage*. 2nd edn. Revised by Sir Ernest Gowers. Oxford: Clarendon Press. (Reprinted 1975.)

Frank, Francine and Anshen, Frank (1983) *Language and the Sexes*. Albany: State University of New York Press.

Frank, Francine and Treichler, Paula A. (eds) (1989) *Language, Gender, and Professional Writing: Theoretical Approaches and Guidelines for Nonsexist Usage*. New York: MLA.

Fry, D.B. (1979) *The Physics of Speech*. Cambridge: Cambridge University Press.

Fudge, Erik (1984) *English Word-Stress*. London: Allen and Unwin.

Gimson, A.C. (1962) *An Introduction to the Pronunciation of English*. London: Edward Arnold.

Gimson, A.C. (1964) 'Phonetic change and the RP vowel system.' In David Abercrombie, D.B. Fry, P.A.D. MacCarthy, N.C. Scott and J.L.M. Trim (eds), *In Honour of Daniel Jones*, London: Longman, pp. 131–6.

Gimson, A.C. (1970) *An Introduction to the Pronunciation of English*. 2nd edn. London: Edward Arnold.

Gimson, A.C. and Ramsaran, Susan (1989) *An Introduction to the Pronunciation of English*. 4th edn. London: Edward Arnold.

Gold, David L. (1977) 'The suffix *-scape*', *American Speech*, **52**, 127.

Gold, David L. (1985) 'Nouns ending in *-mobile*', *American Speech*, **60**, 362–6.

Goldsmith, John A. (1990) *Autosegmental and Metrical Phonology*. Oxford: Blackwell.

Graddol, David and Swann, Joan (1989) *Gender Voices*. Oxford: Blackwell.

Green, Jonathon (1991) *Neologisms*. London: Bloomsbury.

Greenberg, Joseph H. (1966) 'Some universals of grammar with particular reference to the order of meaningful elements.' In Joseph H. Greenberg (ed.), *Universals of Language*, 2nd edn. Cambridge, MA: MIT Press, pp. 73–113.

Guy, Gregory R. and Bayley, Robert (1989) 'On the choice of relative pronouns in English'. Paper presented at NWAVE-XVIII, Durham, N.C., October 1989.

Harris, John (1989) 'Towards a lexical analysis of sound change in progress', *Journal of Linguistics*, **25**, 35–56.

Hartman, James W. (1984) 'Some possible trends in the pronunciation of young Americans (maybe)', *American Speech*, **59**, 218–25.

Henton, C.G. (1983) 'Changes in the vowels of received pronunciation', *Journal of Phonetics*, **11**, 353–71.

Hockett, Charles F. (1958) *A Course in Modern Linguistics*. New York: Macmillan.

Horvath, Barbara M. (1985) *Variation in Australian English. The Sociolects of Sydney*. Cambridge: Cambridge University Press.

Howard, Philip (1977) *New Words for Old*. London: Hamish Hamilton.

Hudson, R.A. (1980) *Sociolinguistics*. Cambridge: Cambridge University Press.

Hudson, R.A. (1987) 'Zwicky on heads', *Journal of Linguistics*, **23**, 109–32.

Jespersen, Otto (1909) *Progress in Language*. London: Swan Sonnenschein and New York: Macmillan.

Johansson, Stig (1979) 'American and British English grammar: an elicitation experiment', *English Studies*, **60**, 195–215.

Johansson, Stig and Hofland, Knut (1989) *Frequency Analysis of English Vocabulary and Grammar*. Oxford: Oxford University Press.

Jones, Daniel (1909) *The Pronunciation of English*. Cambridge: Heffer.

Jucker, Andreas H. (1989) *Stylistic Variation in the Syntax of British Newspaper Language*. Cambridge: Mimeo.

Keenan, Edward L. and Comrie, Bernard (1977) 'Noun phrase accessibility and universal grammar', *Linguistic Inquiry*, **8**, 63–99.

Kelly, John and Local, John (1989) *Doing Phonology*. Manchester and New York: Manchester University Press.

Kikai, Akio, Schleppegrell, Mary and Tagliamonte, Sall (1987) 'The influence of syntactic position on relativization strategies.' In Keith M. Denning, Sharon Inkelas, Faye C. McNair-Knox and John R. Rickford (eds), *Variation in Language: NWAV-XV at Stanford*, Stanford: Department of Linguistics, Stanford University, pp. 266–77.

Kingdon, Roger (1958) *The Groundwork of English Stress*. London: Longmans.

Kisseberth, Charles W. (1970) 'On the functional unity of phonological rules', *Linguistic Inquiry*, **1**, 291–306.

Klima, Edward S. (1964) 'Relatedness between grammatical systems', *Language*, **40**, 1–20. (Reprinted in David A. Reibel and Sanford A. Schane (eds) (1969) *Modern Studies in English*. Englewood Cliffs, NJ: Prentice–Hall, pp. 227–46.)

Kolb, Eduard, Glauser, Beat, Elmer, Willy and Stamm, Renate (1979) *Atlas of English Sounds*. Berne: Francke.

Kroch, Anthony S. (1978) 'Toward a theory of social dialect variation', *Language in Society*, **7**, 17–36.

Kruisinga, E. and Erades, P.A. (1911) *An English Grammar*, 8th edn (1953). Groningen: Noordhoff.

Kučera, Henry and Francis, W. Nelson (1967) *Computational Analysis of Present-Day American English*. Providence, RI: Brown University Press.

Kolin, Philip C. (1979) 'The pseudo-suffix *-holic*', *American Speech*, **54**, 74–6.

Labov, William (1963) 'The social motivation of a sound change', *Word*, **19**, 273–309. (Reprinted in Labov (1972a) pp. 1–42.)

Labov, William (1965) 'On the mechanism of linguistic change.' Reprinted in Labov (1972a) pp. 160–82.

Labov, William (1972a) *Sociolinguistic Patterns*, Philadelphia, PA: University of Pennsylvania Press.

Labov, William (1972b) 'The social setting of linguistic change.' In Labov (1972a) pp. 260–325.

Labov, William (1981) 'Resolving the neogrammarian controversy', *Language*, **57**, 267–308.

Labov, William, Yaeger, Malcah and Steiner, Richard (1972) *A Quantitative Study of Sound Change in Progress*. Philadelphia, PA: US Regional Survey.

Ladefoged, Peter (1975) *A Course in Phonetics*. New York: Harcourt, Brace Jovanovich.

Lakoff, Robin (1972) 'Another look at drift.' In Robert P. Stockwell and Ronald K.S. Macaulay (eds), *Linguistic Change and Generative Theory*, Bloomington and London: Indiana University Press, pp. 172–98.

Lass, Roger (1974) 'Linguistic orthogenesis? Scots vowel quantity and the English length conspiracy.' In John M. Anderson and Charles Jones (eds), *Historical Linguistics II*, Amsterdam: North Holland, pp. 311–52.

Lass, Roger (1984) *Phonology*. Cambridge: Cambridge University Press.

Lass, Roger (1987a) *The Shape of English*. London and Melbourne: J.M. Dent.

Lass, Roger (1987b) 'Language, speakers, history, and drift.' In Willem Koopman, Frederike van der Leek, Olga Fischer and Roger Eaton (eds), *Explanation and Linguistic Change*. Amsterdam and Philadelphia, PA: Benjamins, pp. 151–76.

Leith, Dick (1983) *A Social History of English*. London: Routledge and Kegan Paul.

Lewis, J. Windsor (1969) *A Guide to English Pronunciation*. Oslo: Universitetsforlaget.

Little, Greta D. (1986) 'The ambivalent apostrophe', *English Today*, **8**, 15–17.

Lloyd, Susan M. (ed.) (1982) *Roget's Thesaurus of English Words and Phrases*. Harmondsworth: Penguin.

A Manual of Style (1927) 9th edn. Chicago: Chicago University Press.

A Manual of Style (1969) 12th edn. revised. Chicago and London: Chicago University Press.

Marchand, Hans (1969) *The Categories and Types of Present-Day English Word-Formation*. 2nd edn. Munich: Beck.

Matthews, Richard (1981) ' "The second Great Vowel Shift?"?' *Journal of the International Phonetic Association*, **11**, 22–6.

McArthur, Tom (ed.) (1992) *The Oxford Companion to the English Language*. Oxford and New York: Oxford University Press.

Mencken, H.L. (1936) *The American Language*. 4th edn. New York: Alfred A. Knopf.

Milroy, James (1989) 'The concept of prestige in sociolinguistic argumentation', *York Papers in Linguistics*, **13**, 215–26.

Milroy, James (1992) *Linguistic Variation and Change*. Oxford and Cambridge, MA: Blackwell.

Milroy, James and Milroy, Lesley (1985) *Authority in Language*. London: Routledge and Kegan Paul.

Mohanan, K.P. (1986) *The Theory of Lexical Phonology*. Dordrecht: Reidel.

Montgomery, Michael (1989) 'The standardization of English relative clauses.' In Joseph B. Trahern (ed.), *Standardizing English*. Knoxville: University of Tennessee Press, pp. 113–38.

Mutt, Otto (1967) 'Some recent developments in the use of nouns as premodifiers in English', *Zeitschrift für Anglistik und Amerikanistik*, **15**, 401–8.

Nixon, Graham (1972) 'Corporate concord phenomena in English', *Studia Neo-Philologica*, **44**, 120–6.

Orkin, Mark M. (1971) *Speaking Canadian English*. London: Routledge and Kegan Paul.

Orton, Harold, Sanderson, Stewart, and Widdowson, John (1978) *The Linguistic Atlas of England*. London: Croom Helm.

Pei, Mario (1953) *The Story of English*. London: George Allen and Unwin.

Potter, Simeon (1969) *Changing English*. 2nd edn, revised (1975). London: André Deutsch.

Quirk, Randolph (1957) 'Relative clauses in educated spoken English', *English Studies*, **38**, 97–109.

Quirk, Randolph, Greenbaum, Sidney, Leech, Geoffrey and Svartvik, Jan (1985) *A Comprehensive Grammar of the English Language*. London: Longman.

Ramsaran, Susan (1990) 'RP: fact and fiction.' In Susan Ramsaran (ed.), *Studies in the Pronunciation of English*, London and New York: Routledge, pp. 178–90.

Romaine, Suzanne (1982) *Socio-historical Linguistics*. Cambridge: Cambridge University Press.

Sapir, Edward (1921) *Language*. London: Harvest.

Shnukal, Anna (1981) 'There's a lot mightn't believe this ... variable subject relative pronoun absence in Australian English.' In David Sankoff and Henrietta Cedergren (eds), *Variation Omnibus*. Edmonton: Linguistic Research, pp. 321–8.

Smith, Bernard (1985) *Better Letters*. London: Batsford.

Sommerstein, Alan H. (1977) *Modern Phonology*. London: Edward Arnold.

Stein, Gabriele (1973) *English Word-Formation over Two Centuries*. Tübingen: Gunter Narr.

Strang, Barbara M.H. (1970) *A History of English*. London: Methuen.

Sweet, Henry (1891) *A New English Grammar*. Oxford: Clarendon Press.

Trudgill, Peter (1974a) *The Social Differentiation of English in Norwich*. Cambridge: Cambridge University Press.

Trudgill, Peter (1974b) *Sociolinguistics: an introduction*. Harmondsworth: Penguin.

Trudgill, Peter (ed.) (1978) *Sociolinguistic Patterns in British English*. London: Edward Arnold.

Trudgill, Peter (1986) *Dialects in Contact*. Oxford: Blackwell.

Trudgill, Peter (1988) 'Norwich revisited: recent changes in an English urban dialect', *English World-Wide*, **9**, 33–49.

Trudgill, Peter and Hannah, Jean (1982) *International English*. London: Edward Arnold.

Vennemann, Theo (1975) 'An explanation of drift.' In Charles N. Li (ed.), *Word Order and Word Order Change*, Austin and London: University of Texas Press, pp. 269–305.

Wang, William S-Y. (1969) 'Competing changes as a cause of residue', *Language*, **45**, 9–25.

Wang, William S-Y. (ed.) (1977) *The Lexicon in Phonological Change*. The Hague: Mouton.

Wang, William S-Y. and Chin-Chuan Cheng (1977) 'Implementation of phonological change: the Shuāng-fēng Chinese case.' In Wang (ed.) (1977) pp. 148–58.

Ward, Ida C. (1929) *The Phonetics of English*. Cambridge: Heffer.

Wartburg, W. von (1946) *Évolution et structure de la langue française*. Berne: Francke.

Watson, Bruce (1979) 'The singularity and plurality of collective nouns: a case study', *Melbourne Working Papers in Linguistics*, **5**, 42–9.

Weinreich, Uriel, Labov, William and Herzog, Marvin I. (1968) 'Empirical foundations for a theory of language change.' In W.P. Lehmann and Yakov Malkiel (eds), *Directions for Historical Linguistics*, Austin and London: University of Texas Press, pp. 95–188.

Wells, J.C. (1962) *A Study of the Formants of the Pure Vowels of British English*. Unpublished MA thesis, University College, London.

Wells, J.C. (1982) *Accents of English*. Cambridge: Cambridge University Press.

Werner, Otmar (1987) 'The aim of morphological change is a good mixture – not a uniform language type.' In Anna Giacalone Ramat, Onofrio Carruba and Giuliano Bernini (eds), *Papers from the 7th International Conference on Historical Linguistics*. Amsterdam and Philadelphia, PA: Benjamins, pp. 591–606.

Williams, Raymond (1976) *Keywords*. Revised and expanded, 1983. London: Fontana.

Wurzel, Wolfgang U. (1987) 'System dependent morphological naturalness in inflection.' In Dressler et al., pp. 59–96.

Zwicky, Arnold M. (1985) 'Heads', *Journal of Linguistics*, **21**, 1–29.

Lexica

AHD Morris, William (ed.) (1976) *The American Heritage Dictionary of the English Language*. Boston: Houghton Mifflin.

Barn 1 Barnhart, Clarence L., Steinmetz, Sol and Barnhart, Robert K. (eds) (1973) *The Barnhart Dictionary of New English 1963–1972*. New York: Barnhart and London: Longman.

Barn 2. Barnhart, Clarence L., Steinmetz, Sol and Barnhart, Robert K. (eds) (1980) *The Second Barnhart Dictionary of New English*. Bronxville: Barnhart/Harper and Row.

CDE Hanks, Patrick (ed.) (1979) *Collins Dictionary of the English Language*. London: Collins.

COD 1 Fowler, H.W. and F.G. Fowler (eds) (1911) *The Concise Oxford Dictionary of Current English*. 8th impression, 1920. Oxford: Clarendon Press.

COD 5 Fowler, H.W. and F.G. Fowler (eds) (1911) *The Concise Oxford Dictionary of Current English*. Revised by E. McIntosh. Reprinted with corrections, 1966. Oxford: Clarendon Press.

COD 6 Sykes, J.B. (ed.) (1976) *The Concise Oxford Dictionary of Current English*. 7th impression, 1978. Oxford: Clarendon Press.

COD 7 Sykes, J.B. (ed.) (1982) *The Concise Oxford Dictionary of Current English*. Oxford: Clarendon Press.

COD 8 Allen, R.E. (ed.) (1990) *The Concise Oxford Dictionary of Current English*. Oxford: Clarendon Press.

EPD 1 Jones, Daniel (1917) *An English Pronouncing Dictionary*. London and Toronto: J.M. Dent.

EPD 8 Jones, Daniel (1947) *Everyman's English Pronouncing Dictionary*. London: J.M. Dent. 8th edn, revised with supplement.

EPD 11 Jones, Daniel (1956) *Everyman's English Pronouncing Dictionary*. London: J.M. Dent. 11th edn, completely revised and enlarged.

EPD 14r Jones, Daniel, Gimson, A.C. and Ramsaran, Susan (1988) *Everyman's English Pronouncing Dictionary*. 14th edn, extensively revised and edited by A.C. Gimson, with revisions and supplement by Susan Ramsaran. London and Melbourne: J.M. Dent.

MD Delbridge, A. (ed.) (1981) *The Macquarie Dictionary*. Revised edition, 1985. Dee Why: Macquarie Library.

MDNW   Butler, Susan (1990) *The Macquarie Dictionary of New Words*. Macquarie: Macquarie Library.

ODNW   Tulloch, Sarah (1991) *The Oxford Dictionary of New Words*. Oxford and New York: Oxford University Press.

OED 1   Murray, James H., Bradley, Henry, Craigie, W.A. and Onions, C.T. (eds) (1933) *The Oxford English Dictionary*. Oxford: Clarendon Press. (First published 1884–1928).

OED 2   Simpson, J.A. and Weiner, E.S.C. (eds) (1989) *The Oxford English Dictionary*. 2nd edn. Oxford: Clarendon Press.

OEDS   Burchfield, R.W. (ed.) (1972–86) *A Supplement to the Oxford English Dictionary*. Oxford: Clarendon Press.

PDAE   Kenyon, John Samuel and Knott, Thomas Albert (1944) *A Pronouncing Dictionary of American English*. Springfield, MA: G. and C. Merriam.

RHD   Stein, Jess (ed.) (1967) *The Random House Dictionary of the English Language*. New York: Random House.

Sources of data

AATD   Auswaks, Alex (1980) *A Trick of Diamonds*. London: Collins.

AGNC   Grosu, Alexander (1979) Review of Noam Chomsky, *Essays on Form and Interpretation* (1977), *Journal of Linguistics*, **15**, 356–64.

ALTB   Lindop, A.E. (1976) 'Two bottles of chianti.' In H. Watson (ed.), *Winter's Crimes 8*. London: Macmillan.

AMGC   Maclean, Alistair (1977) *Goodbye California*. London: Collins.

ATZB   Trew, Antony (1975) *The Zhukov Briefing*. London: Collins.

AWGE   Woodbury, Anthony C. (1977) 'Greenlandic Eskimo, ergativity and Relational Grammar', *Syntax and Semantics*, **8**, 307–36.

BBMM   Bova, Ben (1977) *Multiple Man*. London: Gollancz.

CDCB   Dickens, Charles (1874) *Christmas Books*. London: Nelson.

CPSM   Snow, C.P. (1951) *The Masters*. London: Macmillan.

DFAM   Fiske, Dorsey (1980) *Academic Murder*. London: Cassell.

DGCM   Gil, David (1982) 'Case marking, phonological size and linear order', *Syntax and Semantics*, **15**, 117–41.

DLNW   Lodge, David (1988) *Nice Work*. London: Secker and Warburg.

DLSW   Lodge, David (1984) *Small World*. Harmondsworth: Penguin.

DSCT   Shannon, Dell (1978) *Cold Trail*. London: Gollancz.

EMAP McBain, Ed (1986) *Another Part of the City*. London: Hamish Hamilton.

FBAT Bandy, Franklin (1987) *Athena*. New York: Tor.

FHLF Householder, Fred W. (1977) In R.J. Di Pietro and E.L. Blansitt (eds), *The Third LACUS Forum 1976*. Columbia: Hornbeam.

GBPR Bourne, Gordon (1972) *Pregnancy*. London: Cassell.

GMTE Masterton, Graham (1983) *Tengu*. London: Severn House.

GPGP Gazdar, Gerald and Pullam, G.K. (1982) *Generalized Phrase Structure Grammar: a Theoretical Synopsis*. Indiana: Indiana University Linguistics Club.

GSSL Sampson, Geoffrey (1980) *Schools of Linguistics*. London: Hutchinson.

GVHJ Higgins, George V. (1976) *The Judgement of Deke Hunter*. London: Secker and Warburg.

GWEM Wolfe, Gene (1977) 'The eyeflash miracles.' In Terry Carr (ed.), *Best Science Fiction of the Year 6*, London: Gollancz.

HHMS Lambert, J.W. (ed.) (1963) *The Bodley Head Saki*. London: The Bodley Head.

HMCG McCloy, Helen (1976) *Cruel as the Grave*. London: Gollancz.

IAAM Asimov, Isaac (1976) *Authorised Murder*. London: Gollancz.

JADP Anderson, John and Ewen, Colin (1987) *Principles of Dependency Phonology*. Cambridge: Cambridge University Press.

JASM Anderson, John (1979) 'Syntax and the single mother', *Journal of Linguistics*, **15**, 267–87.

JCTP Crosby, John (1986) *Take No Prisoners*. London: Constable.

JETC Ehrlichman, J. (1976) *The Company*. London: Collins.

JIMS Stewart, J.I.M. (1974) *The Gaudy*. London: Gollancz.

JMFF MacDonald, John D. (1981) *Free Fall in Crimson*. London: Collins.

KALJ Amis, Kingsley (1954) *Lucky Jim*. Harmondsworth: Penguin.

KCNP Keenan, Edward L. and Comrie, Bernard (1977) 'Noun phrase accessibility and universal grammar', *Linguistic Inquiry*, **8**, 63–99.

LBTT Block, Lawrence (1984) *The Topless Tulip Caper*. London and New York: Allison and Busby.

LCFH Collins, Larry and Lapierre, Dominique (1980) *The Fifth Horseman*. London: Granada.

LEBS Egan, Lesley (1977) *The Blind Search*. London: Gollancz.

LMCB Mancroft, Lord (1974) *A Chinaman in my Bath and Other Pieces*. London: Bachman and Turner.

LSTG Sanders, Lawrence (1988) *Timothy's Game*. Sevenoaks: NEL.

LUTR Uris, Leon (1976) *Trinity*. London: André Deutsch.

MPTG Peake, Mervin (1946) *Titus Groan*. Harmondsworth: Penguin.

PETP Erdman, Paul (1986) *The Panic of '89*. London: Sphere.

PODM O'Donnell, Peter (1985) *Dead Man's Handle*. London: Souvenir Press.

PPRS Perlmutter, D.M. and Postal, P.M. (1983) 'The relational succession law.' In D.M. Perlmutter and P.M. Postal (eds), *Studies in Relational Grammar 1*. Chicago and London: University of Chicago Press, pp. 30–80.

PP1A Perlmutter, David M. and Postal, Paul M. (1984) 'The 1-Advancement Exclusiveness Law.' In D.M. Perlmutter and Carol G. Rosen (eds), *Studies in Relational Grammar 2*. Chicago: University of Chicago Press, pp. 81–125.

PUDM Ustinov, Peter (1977) *Dear Me*. Harmondsworth: Penguin.

RDBR Duncan, Robert L. (1980) *Brimstone*. London: Michael Joseph.

RHIL Hudson, Richard (1984) *Invitation to Linguistics*. London: Martin Robertson.

RLEC Lass, Roger (1980) *On Explaining Language Change*. Cambridge: Cambridge University Press.

RNZ Radio New Zealand, National Programme.

ROSJ Ormerod, Roger (1987) *The Second Jeopardy*. London: Constable.

RSPU Samek, R. (1965) 'Performative utterances and the concept of contract', *Australasian Journal of Philosophy*, **43**, 196–210.

RTBP Thomas, Ross (1984) *The Briarpatch*. London: Hamish Hamilton.

SJMV Johnson, Stanley (1982) *The Marburg Virus*. London: Heinemann.

SKTS King, Stephen (1978) *The Stand*. London: NEL.

SMCC Marlowe, Stephen (1987) *The Memoires of Christopher Columbus*. London: Jonathan Cape.

SMPD Moody, Susan (1984) *Penny Dreadful*. London: Macmillan.

SSUM Coughlan, John, Lawton, Scott and Weinreb, Glen (1992) *SoundScape User's Manual*. Somerville, MA: GW Instruments.

TGUG Givon, Talmy (1979) *On Understanding Grammar*. New York: Academic Press.

THTR Hoekstra, Teun (1984) *Transitivity*. Dordrecht: Foris.

TPNS   Paikeday, Thomas M. (1985) *The Native Speaker is Dead!* Toronto and New York: PPI.

WDHO   Diehl, William (1984) *Hooligans*. London: Michael Joseph.

WGRA   Garner, William (1984) *Rats' Alley*. London: Heinemann.

WHTM   Haggard, William (1985) *The Meritocrats*. London: Hodder and Stoughton.

Index